The Field Guide to

Lighthouses of the Pacific Coast

California, Oregon, Washington,
Alaska, and Hawai'i

Elinor De Wire

Voyageur Press

Dedication

To Jim Gibbs, for his lifelong dedication to
lighthouse and lightship preservation,
and to Captain Gene Davis for his generosity and support.

First published in 2006 by Voyageur Press, an imprint of MBI Publishing Company,
Galtier Plaza, Suite 200, 380 Jackson Street, St. Paul, MN 55101-3885 USA

The information in this book is true and complete to the best of our knowledge.
All recommendations are made without any guarantee on the part of the author or Publisher,
who also disclaim any liability incurred in connection with the use of this data or specific details.

We recognize, further, that some words, model names, and designations mentioned herein are the
property of the trademark holder. We use them for identification purposes only. This is not an
official publication.

MBI Publishing Company titles are also available at discounts in bulk quantity for industrial or
sales-promotional use. For details write to Special Sales Manager at MBI Publishing Company,
Galtier Plaza, Suite 200, 380 Jackson Street, St. Paul, MN 55101-3885 USA

ISBN-13: 978-0-7603-2466-0
ISBN-10: 0-7603-2466-2

Editor: Kari Cornell
Designer: LeAnn Kuhlmann
Printed in China

On the title page: The quaint cottage-style sentinel at Point Cabrillo, California stands watch
in a pastoral field of wildflowers. The entrance door faces land to protect it from storm winds,
while the two foghorns point seaward. *Elinor De Wire*

On the contents page, clockwise from upper left: At night the bull's eye lens at Point Vicente
Lighthouse creates a distinctive flash as it passes in front of the light source. *Elinor De Wire*

A bright, red lantern tops Yaquina Bay Lighthouse at Newport, Oregon. Discontinued in 1874,
it is now a museum depicting life at a nineteenth century light station. *Jessica De Wire*

The soul of Diamond Head Lighthouse is the opulent third-order Fresnel lens inside its lantern,
casting a welcome beam for vessels arriving in Honolulu. *Jonathan De Wire*

Perforations in the lace-like steps of Yaquina Head Lighthouse and an open railing design allow
air to move freely through the interior of the tower. *Jessica De Wire*

Contents

Acknowledgments

The author is grateful to the following people and organizations for assistance in the preparation of this book: Jeremy D'Entremont, Dr. Robert Browning, Wayne Wheeler, Dave Snyder, Tim Harrison, Kathy Finnegan, Dee Leveille, Sandy Clunies, Dave and Vicki Quinn, the National Archives, Coast Guard Archives, Coast Guard Museum Northwest, and the men and women of the U.S. Coast Guard stations throughout the Pacific who generously provided information and access to sites. Thanks also go to Kari Cornell for her skillful and cheerful editing guidance on this project, and to the crew at Voyageur Press for their professionalism and continuing interest in lighthouses. As always, I am grateful to my family—Jonathan, Jessica, Scott, Kristin, and Rebecca—for their support and encouragement.

Introduction

Lighthouses beguile us with their beauty and romance, their history and lore. During the night, the powerful beams of lighthouses reassure us, banishing the darkness and giving guidance to those who travel uncertain seas. By day, we delight in their marine surroundings and whimsical daymarks of bright colors and bold stripes. It's no wonder poets, painters, and photographers seek inspiration from lighthouses and tourists flock to their doors.

Wayne Wheeler, founder of the San Francisco–based U.S. Lighthouse Society, sums it up well: "Everyone loves lighthouses!" Wheeler sees lighthouses as the quintessential emblems of civility. They offer both a welcome and a warning, and are revered by all for their humanitarian mission. The nonprofit society Wheeler helped charter in 1985 is among hundreds around the nation that endeavor to preserve lighthouses and educate the public about their history and national importance.

Lighthouse preservation is no small mission. In 1915, during the halcyon days of the U.S. Lighthouse Establishment, more than 1,400 lighthouses stood watch along our nation's shores. Today about half that number remain. Some have fallen to the ravages of weather and time, but most are victims of changing technology. Modern forms of navigation using the invisible and silent signals of satellites have lessened the need for lighthouses. The few that remain on duty may someday become altogether obsolete.

Mimicking the nearby Golden Gate Bridge, a wooden suspension span provides safe passage to Point Bonita Lighthouse, which guards the north shore of the entrance to San Francisco Bay. *Elinor De Wire*

Gone as well is the colorful era of the American lighthouse keeper, which can be traced back to 1716 when a colonial beacon went into service at Boston Harbor. Candles produced that first feeble light. The tapers eventually gave way to oil and kerosene lamps, then gas burners, and eventually electricity. During World War I, when lighthouse engineers began experimenting with robotic gadgets, the end of a vibrant era was in sight. Light and sound sensors could do the work of human hands, and they soon began to displace lightkeepers.

In 1939 the U.S. Coast Guard assumed care of the nation's lighthouses. The pace of automation accelerated. Lighthouses were costly to staff and the Coast Guard needed personnel to fill other positions. By the 1960s the push to make lighthouses self-sufficient had become a full-time effort. Under LAMP (Lighthouse Automation and Modernization Program), the Coast Guard evaluated lighthouses one by one, deciding to either discontinue them or automate them. In the early 1990s the last of the American lighthouse keepers retired when Boston Light was de-staffed and handed over to the National Park Service. Lights were switched to automatic operations and padlocks were placed on the tower doors.

The immediate result was a visible compromise of historic integrity. Windows and doors were boarded up, and old classical lenses gave way to plastic optics and solar panels. Eventually the dwellings and towers began to deteriorate or they fell victim to rampant vandalism. Public outcry at the loss of these treasured landmarks produced a groundswell of interest in saving them.

Many lighthouses were added to state and national registers of historic places. Nonprofit groups formed to adopt and care for them. Two large national organizations—the U.S. Lighthouse Society and the American Lighthouse Foundation—took the lead in the preservation effort by spearheading legislation to assure all old lighthouses would be saved. The outcome was the National Historic Lighthouse Preservation Act of 2002. The act transfers ownership of excess Coast Guard lighthouses to worthy private groups and government agencies.

Lighthouses are once again experiencing a heyday. In the past few decades, hundreds have been saved from vandalism and the wrecking ball to become museums or focal points of parks and recreation areas. A new kind of lightkeeper has emerged, one who doubles as a museum docent and park ranger, or a dedicated volunteer eager to share knowledge and open the lighthouse door for visitors. The rescue of our historic sentinels is a symbolic reversal of mission: lighthouses were built to save people, now people are saving lighthouses.

THIS FIELD GUIDE is a roundup of the existing lighthouses along the Pacific Coast of the United States—lighthouses in California, Oregon, Washington, Alaska, and Hawai'i. Most West Coast sentinels still exhibit a beacon each night, while a few serve only as daymarks. Many are favorite destinations for travelers. Their images appear on city seals, business logos, tourist brochures, media advertisements, and a plethora of souvenirs available in gift shops.

In the pages ahead, a short history of lighthouses in each state is followed by an alphabetical listing of those still standing. Each lighthouse is briefly profiled with the nearest town, historical facts of note, directions for finding the lighthouse,

A vintage postcard view of Washington's North Head Lighthouse shows a workroom attached to the tower and two oilhouses. The keepers lived in homes above the site. *Coast Guard Museum NW*

and contacts for further information. Here and there I've sprinkled a few interesting sidebars to provide glimpses into the deeper story of lighthouses. I hope these snapshots of history, along with the individual lighthouse entries, will encourage you to travel to old sentinels of the Pacific Coast. For more information about the lighthouses of the Pacific Coast, refer to the list of online sources and books at the back of this guide.

It's important to note that modern skeleton towers and pole lights are not included in this field guide. There is considerable debate as to what defines a lighthouse, and I will avoid that discussion here. Instead I have chosen to include only what might be called "traditional lighthouses," or those the public would agree are visually attractive and historically significant. These are the wood, masonry, and metal-plate towers, often conical or cottage-style in form and with a noteworthy architectural history. A few skeleton-type towers and ultra-modern lighthouses have been included, due to their historical significance.

As you visit lighthouses on the West Coast, remember to obey no-trespassing signs and to respect private property. Take only pictures, memories, and souvenirs for sale. To add to your enjoyment, you might consider keeping a journal of your lighthouse travels or purchasing a "Lighthouse Passport" from the U.S. Lighthouse Society to record the sites you visit.

Happy lighthouse hunting!

— Elinor De Wire
Seabeck, Washington
2006

Chapter One

———— Lighthouses of California ————

I n 1542, when Portuguese explorer Juan Rodriguez Cabrillo sailed along the coast of present-day California, he probably had no idea a lighthouse would someday bear his name. Point Cabrillo Light near Mendocino is one of more than 30 sentinels that today keep watch over the Golden State's 1,200 miles of coastline.

FOR MORE INFORMATION
U.S. Lighthouse Society
244 Kearny Street
San Francisco, CA 94108
phone 415.362.7255
www.uslhs.org.

Other explorers, traders, whalers, and even pirates followed in Cabrillo's wake, but not until gold was discovered in California in 1848 did anyone think to build a lighthouse. As hundreds of vessels crowded into San Francisco's crude wharf (the staging point for the overland journey to the gold fields), Congress cautiously allocated money to build lighthouses on the West Coast.

A congressional investigation of the U.S. Lighthouse Establishment was ongoing at this time. The 60-year-old agency had come under criticism, accused of being poorly managed and inferior by worldwide standards. The lack of navigational aids on the Pacific Coast was a major downfall of the administration.

By 1852 Congress had addressed these problems with the formation of the U.S. Lighthouse Board, a nine-member committee of military and scientific experts who aimed to overhaul the service and light the West Coast. They set to work immediately, and by June 1, 1854, the first California lighthouse went into operation on Alcatraz Island in San Francisco Bay. It was a Cape Cod–style structure consisting of a simple keeper's dwelling with a tower rising from the roof.

Five more California lighthouses, similar to the first, were completed in 1855, and another four were added the following year. All of the lighthouses exhibited Fresnel lenses. These French-made optics were magnificent aggregates of refracting prisms and magnifying glass held in beehive-shaped brass frames. Oil lamps placed inside the lenses served as the light source. Fresnel lenses were manufactured in various orders, or powers, with first-order lenses being the largest and sixth-order lenses being the smallest. They were state-of-the-art in the nineteenth century and considerably more expensive than other systems for illumination, but their amazing ability to focus and intensify light made them worth the price.

From 1934 until 1969, Alcatraz Island Lighthouse was surrounded by the nation's most notorious criminals. Its keepers felt as if they too were incarcerated. The station was still manned and the prison was still active when this photo was taken in the 1950s. *Coast Guard Museum NW*

Fog signals also were installed at many light stations to augment warnings to mariners when visibility was reduced. Early on, most fog signals were bells, but by 1880 many steam whistles, sirens, and horns also were in use.

California's lightkeepers were hearty stock—men and women who had come from the East Coast by wagon or had made the long journey west by ship, sailing around Cape Horn. Since most light stations were situated in remote places where no roads existed, they were operated as small farms accessible primarily by boat. This allowed the keepers to subsist largely on their own while serving the needs of the shipping industry. To entice them away from the "get rich quick" promise of the Gold Rush, keepers on the Pacific Coast were paid more than their East Coast counterparts.

By the twentieth century the state's chain of navigational aids had grown to more than 40 lighthouses. It included the nation's most expensive lighthouse at St. George Reef and two important lightships anchored off the coasts of San Francisco and Cape Mendocino. California had become known as one of the best-marked coasts in the nation. Other navigation systems, such as radiobeacon and LORAN (Long Range Navigation), further improved light stations. During World War II, light stations became centers of activity for beach patrols and sea watches.

Automation of California's lighthouses began in the 1950s and was completed by 1982. As the lights were unmanned and made self-sufficient, most were adopted by private and civic groups who restored them and opened them to the

public. Today California is the vanguard of American lighthouse preservation, with two-thirds of its sentinels operating as museums or attractions in parks.

The U.S. Lighthouse Society, the first nonprofit group to seek preservation of all lighthouses in the nation, provides information on California lighthouses. It is headquartered in San Francisco.

Automated in 1963, the Alcatraz Light continues to operate by remote control from Fort Point. The once grand keeper's house is now only a shell. *Elinor De Wire*

Alcatraz Island Lighthouse
SAN FRANCISCO

Established in San Francisco Bay in June 1854, Alcatraz Island Lighthouse was the first sentinel to go into service on the West Coast. The cottage-style structure had a short lantern rising from its roof and a third-order fixed Fresnel lens. Two years later the lens was changed to a flashing fourth-order lens.

By 1856, the lighthouse shared the island with a prison whose buildings rose above it. Toward the end of the nineteenth century, the lighthouse deteriorated significantly and a new, taller structure was built. The 84-foot reinforced-concrete tower with an electric arc light went into operation in 1909. The beacon shone from an imposing 214 feet above the bay. Electric fog sirens also were installed on the north and south shores of the island.

FOR MORE INFORMATION
visit www.nps.gov/alcatraz or
e-mail goga_alcatraz@nps.gov

DIRECTIONS
The lighthouse is accessible by boat from Pier 41 near Fisherman's Wharf. The tower is not open for climbing, but visitors touring the prison can go to the base of the lighthouse.

The light was automated in 1963 and currently has a modern flashing optic. The lighthouse is part of Golden Gate National Recreation Area and is operated by remote control from the Coast Guard station at Fort Point.

The first lighthouse on the continental West Coast went into service on Alcatraz Island in San Francisco Bay following the California Gold Rush. *Coast Guard Museum NW*

Anacapa Island Lighthouse
VENTURA

FOR MORE INFORMATION
Channel Islands National Park
1901 Spinnaker Drive
Ventura, CA 93001
805.658.5711
www.nps.gov/chis

DIRECTIONS
Boat tours to the site are
offered through the park
interpretive center at
Channel Island National Park
in Ventura.

Located 14 miles offshore, Anacapa Island Lighthouse has stood watch over Santa Barbara Channel since 1932. The 39-foot tower replaced a gas light mounted on a skeleton tower. The lighthouse originally had a revolving third-order Fresnel lens visible from 25 miles away. Today a modern optic does the job. Two diaphone horns mounted on a foghouse next to the tower sound during periods of fog.

The island became a wildlife refuge in 1938, but Coast Guard families continued to tend the lighthouse until it was automated in 1966. The quarters are now occupied by Channel Islands National Park staff.

Much modernized since its establishment in 1932, the Spanish-style lighthouse at Anacapa Island off Southern California now operates on its own. In 1990, an aerobeacon replaced the Fresnel lens, which is on display in the park. *Courtesy of Derith Bennett*

Battery Point Lighthouse
CRESCENT CITY

A small islet about 200 yards offshore of Crescent City is the site of the 1856 Battery Point Lighthouse. The 45-foot brick tower is incorporated into a small keeper's cottage. The original beacon was a fourth-order flashing Fresnel lens. It served the small port of Crescent City, an entry point to the gold fields and passes of interior Northern California and Oregon.

The lighthouse was automated in 1953 and extinguished in 1965, when a breakwater light took over its duties. In 1982, the Coast Guard gave the lighthouse to the Del Norte Historical Society, which restored and relighted it as a private aid. A caretaker now lives in the lighthouse and opens it for tours.

FOR MORE INFORMATION
Del Norte Historical Society
577 H Street
Crescent City, CA 95531
707.464.3922
www.delnortehistory.org

HOURS OF OPERATION
Wednesday through Sunday,
10 A.M. to 4 P.M.

DIRECTIONS
From US 101 in Crescent City, turn west on Front Street, then south on A Street to a parking area. Take the short walk to the lighthouse at low tide. Consult tide tables to prevent being marooned on the island as the tide rises.

Life at Battery Point Light has always been dictated by the rhythms of the sea. In this 1950s aerial view, the narrow tidal isthmus that separates the station from shore is visible. The lighthouse survived a 1964 tsunami unscathed. *Coast Guard Museum NW*

Right: Battery Point Lighthouse is an example of a Cape Cod–style sentinel. Its New England architect incorporated Puritan simplicity into the design. Numerous additions over the years have lessened its boxlike appearance. *Elinor De Wire*

A Star to Steer By

Red light from the Point Wilson's fourth-order lens glows on the face of Coast Guard lampist Joe Cocking. His 2003 inspection of the 1894 lens deemed it to be in good condition. *Elinor De Wire*

If a lighthouse could be said to possess a soul, it would be the great light pouring from its lantern each night to guide home the lonely mariner. Like a star, it shines dependably and regularly every night. It can beam steadily or it can flash. Its beacon can be white, red to mark a danger area, or red and green to show the port and starboard sides of a channel. Clouds and fog may obscure the beam, but when the skies are clear a lighthouse is a bright star by which to steer.

What makes the great beacon in a lighthouse shine so brightly?

Over the centuries a variety of illuminants and lighting fixtures have been used in lighthouses. The earliest beacons were wood or coal braziers set atop piles of rock. Candelabras with dozens of tapers were hung in the first American lighthouses, followed by pan lamps and spider lamps. These had reservoirs of oil with multiple wicks. Lightkeepers trimmed the wicks frequently to help them burn clean and clear, thus earning the nickname "wickies."

Large individual oil lamps came into use around 1800. These were set in front of silvered reflectors to intensify their light. Circular wicks helped channel air for a more efficient flame. Later, small lenses were positioned in front of the lamps to further magnify the light. Whale oil and fish oil were the most popular fuels, but lard oil and colza oil (made from cabbage) also were used.

Until the 1820s all lights were white and fixed, and they seldom could be seen more than a few miles away. There was no technology to make them flash. This changed when French physicist Augustin-Jean Fresnel developed a revolutionary lenticular system. He placed mirrors and prisms around an oil lamp to bend and focus its light into a bright ray. His magnificent apparatus could transform an oil lamp's weak light into a piercing beam visible as far as 300 miles at sea.

Fresnel built lenses in six sizes, called orders. A large first-order lens served a seacoast light, while a small sixth-order lens was suitable for a river beacon. Later, titanic hyperradiant lenses were developed for important landfall lights. Fixed lenses had a smooth barrel of magnifying glass, while flashing lenses were composed of a series of magnifying bull's eyes that broke the light into individual beams. These appeared to flash as the lens revolved, and, if timed properly, gave the lighthouse a unique signal.

Fresnel lenses were heavy and turned on bearings or chariot wheels. Larger models floated on a thin layer of mercury—a low-friction, high-density element. A clockwork system with weights suspended in the

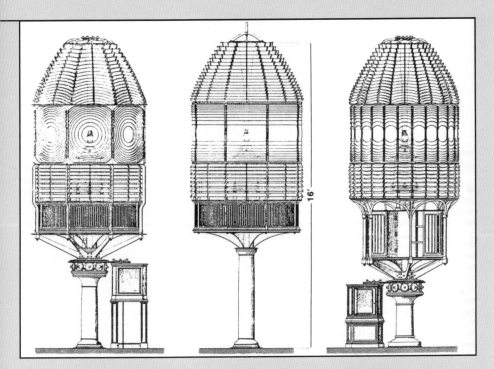

Fresnel lenses were fixed (center) and flashing (left and right). Bull's eyes created flashes while a smooth, central drum produced a fixed light. A variety of methods were used to rotate the light, including chariot wheels. *U.S. Lighthouse Society*

tower, similar to a cuckoo clock mechanism, kept the lens revolving at a specified rate. The keepers wound up the weights every few hours. As the weights fell, the lens turned. During the day, keepers spent a considerable amount of time cleaning the lens and maintaining the gears of the clockworks.

Oil lamps as light sources were replaced by incandescent oil vapor lamps in the 1880s, and by acetylene gas lamps in the 1890s. When electricity came to lighthouses early in the twentieth century, the old Fresnel lenses were upgraded to operate with electric lightbulbs. In the 1960s, automation ushered in smaller, more durable plastic lenses that worked on the same principle as the classic Fresnels. Plastic lens housings required little care and could be exposed to the weather.

Myriad sensors and timers were devised to turn the lights on and off and rotate replacement lightbulbs into position when old ones burned out. Solar panels replaced external power sources at many remote lighthouses. This progress has rendered all active lighthouses self-sufficient and made the job of the live-in lightkeeper obsolete. Coast Guard Aids to Navigation Teams (ANTs) still visit lighthouses every few months to check the automatic equipment. In a sense, they are lightkeepers, though their services are minimal and they need not live on-site.

Lighthouses have become robots, able to run themselves.

Cape Mendocino Lighthouse
FERNDALE

DIRECTIONS
From US 101 about 2 miles north of Garberville, turn west at the sign for Shelter Cove. Drive 25 miles to Ferndale and the Humboldt County Fairgrounds, where the lighthouse now sits.

California's westernmost point is home to Cape Mendocino Lighthouse. It was opened in December 1868 with a first-order revolving Fresnel lens. The short tower, constructed of iron plates, was perched 422 feet above the ocean and aided ships making a critical course change north of San Francisco.

The station experienced many severe storms over the years, with damage to the keepers' dwellings, but the iron tower stood firm. The light was extinguished in 1951 and the beacon was placed on a pole near the tower. Earthquake damage in 1992, along with vandalism, nearly spelled an end for the old tower.

In 1998 the lighthouse was dismantled and transported by helicopter to Shelter Cove for restoration. It now serves as an exhibit on the town's shorefront.

Cape Mendocino Light was staffed and active when this photo was taken in 1945. A white curtain was drawn around the lens to protect it. The small shack was for watch standers who maintained a constant vigil over the coast during the war. *U.S. Navy*

East Brother Light Station
RICHMOND

The quaint Victorian lighthouse on East Brother Island, about a half-mile from Point Richmond, has stood watch over the entrance to San Pablo Strait since March 1874. The 48-foot wooden tower was incorporated into the keeper's house. A fourth-order flashing Fresnel lens casts a beam about 10 miles over the bay.

Three months after the light went into service a steam whistle was installed to penetrate the fog. Water for the whistle was brought at first by ship; later, a cement cistern that took up most of the island was built to supply the water.

In 1967 the station was automated with a modern, self-sufficient beacon. A few years later the station was restored and opened as a bed and breakfast. It is accessible by boat for day trips or overnight stays.

FOR MORE INFORMATION
East Brother Light Station
117 Park Place
Point Richmond, CA 94801
510.233.2385
Visit www.ebls.org or
e-mail info@ebls.org for
reservations for a daytrip
or an overnight stay.

DIRECTIONS
For directions to the boat dock
in Point Richmond visit
www.ebls.org.

The handsome Victorian lighthouse at East Brother Island, automated in 1970, has found a new life as a posh B&B. *Elinor De Wire*

Farallon Island Lighthouse
SAN FRANCISCO

FOR MORE INFORMATION
To find out more about boat
tours and to obtain directions
to the boat dock, contact:
Oceanic Society Expeditions
Fort Mason Center
San Francisco, CA 94123
800.326.7491
www.oceanicsociety.org

The Farallon Islands are about 23 miles off the coast of San Francisco. The name means "brothers" in Spanish. A squat, brick lighthouse went into operation on the summit of southeast Farallon Island in 1855, more than 200 feet above sea level. Quarters for the keepers were built below it.

A first-order Fresnel lens casts a beam about 20 miles seaward. The island's first fog signal was a train whistle mounted over a natural blowhole and was actuated by the concussion of air. It proved unreliable and was replaced by a steam siren in 1882.

The station was automated in 1972 with a modern optic. Today it is part of the Point Reyes Farallon Island National Marine Sanctuary. Though the island is off-limits to visitors, special tour boats visit the waters around the island on weekends from June through November.

Lightkeepers at remote Farallon Light relied on pack mules with names like Jerry, Paddy, and Jack to haul supplies from the dock up a long switchback trail to the tower.
Nautical Research Center

Fort Point Lighthouse
SAN FRANCISCO

Beneath the south side of the Golden Gate Bridge is the diminutive Fort Point Lighthouse. The steel tower perches on the fort's northwest wall but is no longer an active beacon. It was discontinued in 1937 when lights and foghorns on the bridge deck superseded it.

The first sentinel located here was a cottage-style design with a lantern rising from the roof. While awaiting delivery of its lens in 1854, construction of a fort began on the site. The lighthouse was torn down and a wooden light tower was erected between the fort and the bay. It became operational with a fifth-order Fresnel lens in March 1855.

After erosion destroyed the wooden tower, the third and current lighthouse was built on the fort wall in 1864. The modest 27-foot tower is part of Fort Point National Historic Site.

FOR MORE INFORMATION
Fort Point NHS
Fort Mason, Building 201
San Francisco, CA 94123
415.556.1693
www.nps.gov/fopo

HOURS OF OPERATION
Open daily, 10 A.M. to 5 P.M.

DIRECTIONS
From Lincoln Boulevard in San Francisco, turn north at Long Avenue and follow signs to the Fort Point National Historic Site.

Nestled beneath the brightly lighted Golden Gate Bridge, diminutive Fort Point Lighthouse no longer signals to vessels entering San Francisco Bay. ©2003 Ed Litfin

Four-Footed Keepers

Few lighthouse families were without pets. Animals eased the loneliness of isolated duty and provided important services.

Cats kept down the rodent population—no small service considering the many wooden buildings at light stations. Their natural agility allowed them to climb the towers without fear and dispatch bugs drawn to the light. Island felines swam to shore to visit other cats or stowed away on supply ships that visited the stations. Sometimes the receding tide influenced the cat's urge to roam. The cats at Battery Point Lighthouse made their trips to shore only at low tide, when the isthmus separating the lighthouse from the mainland was no longer covered by water. With amazing regularity, the cats always returned before the tide came in.

Dogs were indispensable. They guarded the light stations, watching for a ship in distress, an intruder, a child in danger. Large breeds, such as Newfoundlands, were prized for their love of water and their rescue skills. In the 1920s a dog at Cape Flattery Lighthouse swam out to fetch the mail from the canoe-paddling carrier. His courage often averted disaster for "Lighthouse Charley," the postman from the Makah Reservation since, even on calm days, Charley's canoe could be smashed on the rocks rimming the island.

Smaller dogs had important roles too. Most were good ratters and discouraged seabirds from landing and fouling the buildings. Anacapa Island Lighthouse had as many as 13 dogs in the 1950s, mostly beagles with a special mission. The hounds must have thought they were in rabbit heaven. A pair of pet Belgian hares had escaped from the house years before, multiplied, and overran the island, digging holes everywhere. The dogs eradicated the rabbits, and the keepers filled in the holes.

Dogs sometimes served the keepers in even more peculiar ways. At Yaquina Head Lighthouse in the 1920s, assistant keeper Frank Story only went into the tall tower when accompanied by his bulldog. He felt the dog would protect him from the ghost of another keeper who had died in the tower.

The most critical animals at lighthouses were those with hoofs and feathers. Cows and goats did their share to provide the lighthouse children with milk and cheese. Goats kept the brush and grass at a manageable height. Chickens provided meat and eggs, a vital service when the supply ship was unable to land. Horses, mules, and oxen not only helped build the stations but often stayed on to serve the keepers in a variety of ways. These large animals were transported to island lighthouses by a supply ship and were lifted in a sling onto the dock at their new home. The experience was traumatic, leaving the beleaguered beasts seasick and bawling, but grateful to have their feet on dry land once again.

At Farallon Island Lighthouse a steep switchback trail led from the boat dock to the lighthouse. Mules helped in the construction of the station, and one was left on site to serve the keepers. The station mule pulled provisions to the homes and coal to the foghouse, then backpacked oil and tools to the tower.

One of the best-known Farallon mules was Jerry, a smart character who always heard the whistle of the supply ship long before his human owners did. Its distant, shrill cry usually sent Jerry hastily retreating to the far end of the island to hide, since he knew the arrival of the ship meant work was at hand. Jerry was much loved by the lighthouse children, who rode him over the island trails and dressed him in funny hats. When he died he was buried on Farallon Island the lightkeepers cried as if one of their own had passed on.

Companionship was a critical part of life at lighthouses. A Coast Guard couple at Cape Flattery Lighthouse felt it was important to include their dog in this photo from around 1960. *Coast Guard Archives*

Long Beach Harbor Lighthouse
LONG BEACH

This modern sentinel, nicknamed "The Robot," marks the center of the 2-mile-long breakwater at San Pedro Harbor. It works in tandem with Los Angeles Harbor Light to guide shipping safely into busy Los Angeles Harbor. Built in 1949 and fully automatic, it is one of the newer lights on the West Coast. It stands 42 feet tall and is an art deco–style tower. The beacon and fog signal operate continuously.

The lighthouse sits on the end of a breakwater and is not accessible from shore. It can be seen from several vantage points in Long Beach.

Designed to allow wind and waves to pass through unimpeded, the original Long Beach Breakwater Light was a skeleton design. It was replaced by the current "Robot Light" in 1949. *Coast Guard Archives*

Los Angeles Harbor Lighthouse
LOS ANGELES

Perched on a concrete platform at the end of the 2-mile-long San Pedro Breakwater, Los Angeles Harbor Lighthouse leads the way to the West Coast's largest port. It was built in 1913 and is sometimes called Angel's Gate Lighthouse. The tower, constructed of steel columns and plates covered in cement, was painted in contrasting panels of black and white. A fourth-order Fresnel lens illuminated by an incandescent oil vapor lamp served as the beacon. Compressed-air sirens were used as the fog signal.

DIRECTIONS
The lighthouse is not accessible from shore but can be viewed from a beach pier off Stephen M. White Street.

The lighthouse was automated in 1973. A decade later, the beacon became the first lighthouse on the West Coast to be powered by the sun. Its Fresnel lens was removed and given to the Los Angeles Maritime Museum.

Jeremy D'Entremont Collection

When it was built in 1913, Los Angeles Harbor Light was state-of-the-art. Its steel construction has withstood several severe earthquakes and a collision by a Navy battleship. *Coast Guard Archives*

Piedras Blancas Lighthouse
CAMBRIA

DIRECTIONS
At present the lighthouse is inaccessible. It can be viewed from Highway 1, one mile north of the entrance to San Simeon State Park.

To close the long, dark space between Point Pinos and Point Conception, a 115-foot tower was built in 1875 at Piedras Blancas. The tower exhibited a first-order Fresnel lens. A handsome duplex for the keepers completed the station.

In 1906 a fog signal was added. After the Coast Guard took control of the lighthouse in 1939, a storm damaged the lantern and it had to be removed. An exposed aerobeacon was installed atop the tower. The lens was given to the Cambria County Lions Club and is displayed in a faux lantern on the Pinedorado grounds in Cambria.

The station was automated in 1975. Currently the Bureau of Land Management is restoring the station and plans to open it to the public.

Prior to 1948, when a storm damaged the top of Piedras Blancas Lighthouse, it had an ornate lantern. This image from the early 1900s shows the station in its halcyon days. *Bureau of Land Management*

A young lightkeeper from Piedras Blancas Lighthouse is pictured in his uniform. *Bureau of Land Management*

Pigeon Point Light Station
PESCADERO

FOR MORE INFORMATION
HI-Pigeon Point Lighthouse
210 Pigeon Point Road
Pescadero, CA 94060
e-mail
pplhostel@norcalhostels.org
www.norcalhostels.org/pigeon

DIRECTIONS
The station can be easily
spotted 5 miles south of the
Pescadero turnoff from
Highway 1.

Named for the clipper ship *Carrier Pigeon*, which wrecked off the point in 1853, stately Pigeon Point Lighthouse went into service in 1873 to provide a first-order seacoast guide for vessels headed north to San Francisco. The 115-foot tower shares the distinction of being the tallest tower on the West Coast with Point Arena Lighthouse. Its original layout included a quadraplex Victorian house for the keepers and a whistle house for the fog signal. The Coast Guard razed the dwelling and replaced it with bungalows in the 1960s.

The lighthouse was automated in 1979 and shortly after it was licensed to the California Department of Parks and Recreation. Hostelling International/American Youth Hostels operates the station as a hostel for travelers.

PIGEON POINT LIGHT

In 1910, Hassan Cigarette Company began offering lighthouse cards in packs of cigarettes. An image of Pigeon Point Lighthouse was among these collectibles.
Elinor De Wire Collection

Lofty Pigeon Point Lighthouse is one the brightest on the Pacific Coast. Its 9-foot-tall, first-order lens is visible more than 20 miles at sea. A curtain protects the lens in the daytime. In 1883, a lightkeeper told a group of visitors that if he drew back the curtain, heat from the giant lens would cook their flesh. The ploy was intended to prevent fingerprints, which the keeper would have been required to clean. *Elinor De Wire*

Point Arena Lighthouse
POINT ARENA

FOR MORE INFORMATION
Point Arena Lighthouse Keepers
P.O. Box 11
Point Arena, CA 95468
toll-free 877.725.4448
e-mail palight@mcn.org
www.mcn.org/1/palight

DIRECTIONS
From Highway 1 at Rollerville Junction in Point Arena, turn west and take Lighthouse Road to the site.

Point Arena is a landmark for ships headed south into San Francisco. Its original lighthouse, a 100-foot-tall brick tower built in 1870, had a first-order fixed Fresnel lens. The quadraplex keeper's dwelling sat near the tower and a steam whistle served in periods of fog. The station was destroyed in the 1906 earthquake.

A reinforced-concrete tower, 115 feet tall, was built the following year. The first-order Fresnel lens from the original tower was installed in the new tower. In the 1960s, Coast Guard bungalows replaced the old keeper's house. The light was automated with a modern aerobeacon in 1977. Today the bungalows are vacation rentals.

Dual bulbs are visible through concentric rings of magnifying glass in a bull's eye of the first-order lens at Point Arena Lighthouse. The heavy lens once floated in mercury to ease rotation. *Elinor De Wire*

The slender column of Point Arena Lighthouse is designed to withstand earthquake shocks. The reinforced concrete tower has a low center of gravity and can sway several inches without harm. **Left:** *Coast Guard Museum NW* **Above:** *Elinor De Wire*

Point Bonita Lighthouse
SAN FRANCISCO

FOR MORE INFORMATION
www.nps.gov/goga/mahe/pobo

HOURS OF OPERATION
Tours are offered Saturday
through Monday, 12:30 P.M.
to 3:30 P.M.

DIRECTIONS
On the north side of the Golden
Gate Bridge, take the
Alexander Avenue exit to Marin
Headlands, then drive through
a tunnel and onto Conzelman
Road, following signs to the
Point Bonita parking area. Walk
1 mile to the lighthouse.

Perched on precipitous cliffs 306 feet above the sea, the 56-foot Point Bonita Lighthouse began service in 1855. It exhibited a second-order Fresnel lens. The fog signal was a cannon fired twice an hour. Too arduous to operate, it was later replaced by a bell.

Erosion and landslides destroyed the station. It was rebuilt in 1877 on a rock ledge 124 feet above the sea. A small bridge connected the lighthouse to shore and a tunnel led to the keepers' homes on the cliff. A new dwelling and fog signal were constructed in 1915. The station was automated in 1981 and transferred from the Coast Guard to the Golden Gate National Recreation Area.

Sentry for the Golden Gate, the lens
of Point Bonita Light was the last in
California to be automated. Handholds
visible on the exterior window frames
allowed keepers to safely clean the glass
on windy days. *Elinor De Wire*

Right: Shining a welcome light to ships
entering San Francisco Bay, Point Bonita
Light perches on a rock outcropping.
It is reached by a tunnel and a wooden
suspension bridge. *Elinor De Wire*

Point Cabrillo Light Station
MENDOCINO

Built in 1909, the Point Cabrillo lighthouse lit a dark gap on the Mendocino coast. The wooden tower, incorporated into an air-siren foghouse, resembled a small country church. Its third-order flashing Fresnel lens was decommissioned in 1972, but was reactivated by the North Coast Interpretive Association in 1999. The group manages the station, which has a gift shop in the foghouse and vacation rentals in the keepers' dwellings.

FOR MORE INFORMATION
North Coast Interpretive
Association
P.O. Box 641
Mendocino, CA 95460
e-mail info@pointcabrillo.org
www.pointcabrillo.org

HOURS OF OPERATION
Daily, 9 A.M. to 6 P.M.

DIRECTIONS
Two miles north of Mendocino on Highway 1, turn onto Point Cabrillo Road at Russian Gulch. Follow signs to the lighthouse.

Bathed in the evening glow, the lighthouse at Point Cabrillo resembles a country church. While its lens still casts a beam over the Mendocino Coast, the fog signal machinery inside has been replaced by a gift shop. *Elinor De Wire*

Point Conception Lighthouse
SANTA BARBARA

Nicknamed the "Cape Horn of the Pacific," Point Conception is a critical turning point for ships plying the California coast. Its first lighthouse, a cottage-style sentinel with a first-order lens, was built in 1855 on a high bluff on the point. The fog signal was a bell, which was replaced by a steam whistle in 1872.

Storms battered the lighthouse, and it had to be rebuilt in 1882. A granite base and brick walls strengthened the new 52-foot tower and foghouse. Comfortable keepers' homes were added in 1906, and the station was automated in 1973. It continues to operate today but is not accessible to the public.

Marking an important turn in the West Coast shipping route, Point Conception Lighthouse perches on a remote 133-foot-high bluff. The huge first-order lens, which served throughout the station's long career, was not electrified until 1948. *Courtesy of Derith Bennett*

Point Fermin Lighthouse
Los Angeles

A beacon for San Pedro Bay, the Carpenter Gothic sentinel at Point Fermin operated from 1874 to 1941. Women tended the lighthouse through much of its career. The lighthouse was occupied by the army during World War II, and later became a residence for Los Angeles City park personnel.

Restoration efforts began in the 1980s. The lighthouse's exterior and grounds have been restored and the interior serves as a museum. The Point Fermin chapter of the U.S. Lighthouse Society administers the site and holds tours on Sundays.

FOR MORE INFORMATION
U.S. Lighthouse Society,
Point Fermin Chapter
366 South Hamilton Avenue
San Pedro, CA 90732

HOURS OF OPERATION
Tours offered on Sunday,
1 P.M. to 4 P.M.

DIRECTIONS
From I-110 South, take the Gaffey Street exit and proceed to Point Fermin Park.

The handsome Carpenter Gothic–style lighthouse at Point Fermin was built of redwood and fir. Women tended the light through much of its career. The last lady keeper was young Thelma Austin who felt she had "a scared duty to perform." She retired in 1927, but survived to celebrate the lighthouse's centennial in 1974. *Elinor De Wire*

Point Hueneme Lighthouse
PORT HUENEME

DIRECTIONS
From Highway 1 in Oxnard, turn west on Port Hueneme Road. Follow signs for the lighthouse.

The 52-foot concrete moderne tower and integrated fog signal house at Point Hueneme was built in 1941 to replace a Victorian-style lighthouse established in 1874 that exhibited a fourth-order Fresnel lens. The Victorian light served until dredging began for Port Hueneme in 1939, at which point it was sold and eventually razed. The new lighthouse went into service at a more useful location. It remains in operation as part of a city park.

The World War II–era, modern light tower at Point Hueneme provides critical service to mariners. As recently as 1970, a shipwreck occurred in the vicinity when the 465-foot liner *LaJannelle* was driven ashore in a storm. *Elinor De Wire*

Point Loma Light Station (Old)
SAN DIEGO

Established in 1855 on a promontory enclosing San Diego Harbor, the Point Loma lighthouse was a cottage-style sentinel. It shone from 462 feet above sea level and had a third-order Fresnel lens. While its lofty beacon was visible as far away as 35 miles, winter fogs obscured the light. Still, no fog signal was installed.

Complaints about fog prompted the construction of two additional lighthouses—one at Ballast Point in 1890 and one on the beach on the west side of the promontory. Point Loma Lighthouse was abandoned in 1892 and stood derelict until the 1930s, when it was restored as the centerpiece of Cabrillo National Monument.

A third-order lens was put back in the tower, and today it shines as a memorial light. Exhibits of the site's history are housed inside the tower and in the nearby interpretive center.

FOR MORE INFORMATION
Cabrillo National Monument
1800 Cabrillo Memorial Drive
San Diego, CA 92106
619.557.5450
www.nps.gov/cabr

HOURS OF OPERATION:
Interpretive center open
daily, 9 A.M. to 5 P.M.

DIRECTIONS
Where I-8 and I-5 intersect
north of central San Diego,
take the Rosecrans Street
(Highway 209) exit, then follow
signs to Point Loma.

Built too high above the sea, Old Point Loma's beacon failed to reach ships in San Diego's occasional low fogs. Keeper Robert Israel's only fog signal was his shotgun, which he fired if he sighted a ship too close to shore. Eventually, the lighthouse was re-established at a lower elevation.
Elinor De Wire

Point Loma Light Station (New)
SAN DIEGO

FOR MORE INFORMATION
See Point Loma Lighthouse
(Old)

DIRECTIONS
Inside Cabrillo National Monument, take Cabrillo Road to the lighthouse. The lighthouse is not open and the grounds are private, but there is ample viewing area outside the fence.

In March 1891 a skeleton-tower lighthouse replaced the defunct cottage-style light on the summit of Point Loma. The tower's opulent third-order Fresnel lens shone through windowpanes of ruby glass. Two Victorian homes for the keepers were built behind the tower.

The station was given a fog signal in 1913 to deal with persistent fogs in winter and spring. A fog signal keeper came to the station, and a new house was built for his family. That same year, the red panels in the lantern were removed and the light flashed white.

A radiobeacon was added in the 1920s and electricity came to the station in 1926. The station was automated with a modern optic in the 1980s. The Fresnel lens was moved to the exhibit center at Cabrillo National Monument.

Skeleton towers were durable, inexpensive, and easy to build. Wind and waves passed through the iron legs. New Point Loma Light was state of the art in 1891. *Collection of Elinor De Wire*

THE SOCIALITE LIGHTKEEPER

Lighthouse keeping was, by and large, an arduous occupation held by men. They designed the light-houses and built, tended, and repaired them. When lightkeepers died, sometimes their wives or daughters were given the job. It was easier to appoint a widow or other female relative than to train a new man, and cheaper because women seldom earned equal pay. Yet, in this male-dominated world, a few unusual ladies rose to prominence. Emily Fish was one of them.

Mrs. Fish learned social graces as a girl in Michigan and she married well. Her physician husband practiced medicine in China for many years and returned to the United States in 1862 with Emily and their daughter Julia. He attended the sick and injured during the Civil War as a Union officer, then was transferred to the Army installation at Benecia in San Francisco.

When he died in 1893, fifty-year-old Emily began to look for activities to fill her time. There were always charities in need of help—a wealthy widow would have been expected to do volunteer work—or she could open a millinery or dress shop. But Mrs. Fish set her sights on something more engaging. Her son-in-law, Henry Nichols, was the lighthouse district inspector in California. He soon made arrange-ments for her to have the lightkeeping job at Point Pinos Lighthouse in Monterey. She took charge of the station on June 29, 1893, and remained on duty for 21 years.

During those years she gained a reputation not only as an excellent lighthouse keeper but also a Monterey socialite. Mrs. Fish planted beautiful gardens at the lighthouse and kept champion livestock, which her Chinese servant helped her tend. She held teas and dinners in her home, and when she drove her carriage into town to attend a high-society event, a French poodle sat on a velvet cushion beside her.

Emily was always fashionably dressed, even as she went about her lighthouse duties. She wrote verbose entries in her logbook describing the lighthouse work, but she also wrote about such things as rainbows, meteor showers, and the appearance of Halley's Comet in 1910. On May 8, 1906, she wrote a terse but clear entry about the earthquake that had rocked the station: "Earthquake at 11:40 p.m., quite severe. Lens, etc. jostled, rattled, and jingled."

Lightkeeping must have been in the family genes, for after Mrs. Fish's daughter was widowed, she also became a lightkeeper and served many years at Angel Island Light in San Francisco Bay. Like her mother, she was dedicated to her work. On one occasion when the fogbell striker broke down, Julia rang the bell by hand for several days until a repairman arrived to fix the striker.

Mrs. Fish retired in 1914 with a Letter of Commendation from the Department of Commerce. She and Que, her Chinese servant, moved to a quiet home in Pacific Grove. She died at the age of 88 and is buried in Oakland with her daughter and son-in-law.

Few lightkeepers were as dignified and refined as Emily Fish. She brought a touch of class to an otherwise homespun occupation. *Monterey Public Library*

Point Montara Station
MONTARA

FOR MORE INFORMATION
Write the hostel manager
HI-Point Montara Lighthouse
Attn: Hostel Manager
P.O. Box 737
Montara, CA 94037
e-mail
himontara@norcalhostels.org
www.norcalhostels.org/montara

HOURS OF OPERATION
Visiting hours for the
lighthouse vary and are
posted at the entrance to the
hostel. The grounds are open
daily, 7:30 A.M. to 9:30 A.M.
and 4:30 P.M. to 9:30 P.M.

DIRECTIONS
The lighthouse is easily spotted
from Highway 1 between
Montara and Moss Beach.

Heavy fogs spurred the 1875 construction of a steam whistle on Point Montara, about 25 miles south of San Francisco. In 1900 a small post light was added to the site, and it was changed to a fourth-order lens in a wooden framework tower in 1912. A 30-foot cast-iron tower replaced the wooden tower in 1928.

The lighthouse was automated in 1970, and its classical lens went on display at San Mateo County Historical Museum. The fog signal machinery was shut down and an off-shore buoy took over its duties. In the 1980s a hostel opened in the keeper's quarters. A small display is housed in the old fog signal building.

The keeper's quarters (right) at Point Montara Lighthouse were made into a hostel in the 1980s. Switch-dorm style rooms accommodate budget travelers. A small exhibit is housed in the old fog signal building, seen in the center.
Elinor De Wire

Opposite: *Coast Guard Museum NW*

Point Pinos Lighthouse
PACIFIC GROVE

FOR MORE INFORMATION
831.648.5716 ext.13
www.pgmuseum.org/
Lighthouse.htm

HOURS OF OPERATION
The museum is open in
winter Thursday through
Monday, 1 P.M. to 4 P.M.
Extended hours are offered
in summer.

DIRECTIONS
From Highway 1 in Monterey,
turn west on SR 68. Take
Sunset Drive, then turn right
on Asilomar Avenue. Follow
signs to the lighthouse.

The oldest continuously operating lighthouse on the West Coast is the little sentinel at Point Pinos. It went into service in 1855 with a third-order lens fueled by oil lamps. The lighthouse was jolted by the 1906 San Francisco earthquake, which rocked the lens and sent a crack up the tower wall. The structure was repaired by the Lighthouse Board and electrified 12 years later. When the lighthouse was automated in 1975, the Pacific Grove Historical Society began operating it as a museum. The tower's third-order lens still shines over the bay, but also over a modern golf course.

A groomed lawn and gardens highlight an early postcard view of Point Pinos Lighthouse. Its keepers took great pride in maintaining the station in apple-pie order. *Elinor De Wire Collection*

Point Reyes Light Station
POINT REYES STATION

Considered one of the foggiest and windiest places on the West Coast, Point Reyes was marked with a lighthouse in 1870. The squat cast-iron tower showed a first-order beacon from a ledge 294 feet above sea level. A fog signal building sat next to the tower and a comfortable duplex for the keepers was built on the summit above the lighthouse.

The station saw a series of changes in technology and personnel until automation in 1975, when a modern optic and electric foghorns were installed. The lighthouse then became the centerpiece of Point Reyes National Seashore.

Light-station exhibits are housed in the Bear Valley Interpretive Center at Point Reyes Station. Visitors access the lighthouse and fog signal building via a 300-step staircase (with rest areas).

FOR MORE INFORMATION
Point Reyes National Seashore Association
Point Reyes Station, CA 94956
415.663.1224
www.ptreyes.org

HOURS OF OPERATION
Tours of the light station are offered Thursday through Monday, 10 A.M. to 4:30 P.M. Tours are cancelled during high winds.

DIRECTIONS
From US 101 or Highway 1 north of San Francisco, take the Sir Francis Drake Boulevard exit and follow signs to Point Reyes National Seashore and the parking area for the lighthouse.

Fog envelopes precipitous Point Reyes Light as visitors descend the long staircase on a July morning. Summer days here are often cold due to persistent wind and fog. *Elinor De Wire*

Lightkeepers peer over the cliff at Point Reyes Light in the 1890s. The stubby tower sits nearly 300 feet above the sea. *Coast Guard Archives*

Fog Sounds

Fog signaling work was as important at lighthouses as keeping the light. When the air became thick and the light failed to shine the necessary distance, sound became the seaman's guide. Though a boon for ships, it meant hours of hard work and incessant noise for lighthouse families.

Fog seldom plagued Hawai'i, but Northern California and the Pacific Northwest were socked-in as much as a quarter of the year. San Francisco is renowned for its fog. A symphony of bongs, chimes, honks, and roars sing to the seamen when the murk rolls into the bay. Point Reyes Light, a few miles north of the city, often held the fog record. Its horns blared roughly three days out of five. Many of Puget Sound's sentinels started their careers as fog signal stations and later segued into light stations. Alaskan lighthouses dealt with ice fogs and what lightkeepers called "sea smoke," a thick fog that

A variety of contraptions were tested for use as fog signals. At Boston Light in the 1870s, a fog trumpet magnified the sound of a reed horn. *National Archives*

not only obscured the light but also played devious tricks with sound signals.

A variety of devices and methods were tested to penetrate the fog. The first keeper at Old Point Loma Lighthouse in San Diego fired his shotgun at regular intervals when fog descended on the promontory. A cannon was set up at Point Bonita Lighthouse in the 1850s, but the cost for shot was high and the sound carried poorly over the sea. Also, it was difficult to find a keeper willing to do the work.

Bells came into use in 1820 and were rung by hand, taking up much of the keeper's time and energy. Vibration from larger bells sometimes caused paint to loosen from walls and jiggled cups in the kitchen cupboard, not to mention disturbing sleep. The huge bell at Ediz Hook Lighthouse in Washington set all the metal parts of the light station sympathetically humming. The manual drudgery of fogbells was eased in the 1870s when bell-striking mechanisms came into use. The work then consisted of winding up weights in the bell tower every few hours so that the bell's clockworks would run the striker.

Most West Coast lighthouses used steam whistles, horns, or sirens as fog signals. A California lightkeeper inspects two horns for problems. Sand blew inside the horns, or sometimes seabirds nested in them in summer when there was little fog. *Nautical Research Center*

Steam-powered fog signals were also in use by this time, including whistles, sirens, and horns mounted on steam boilers. The familiar two-tone nasal honk of the diaphone horn came along in the 1870s, and the multitoned diaphragm horn arrived a decade later. For the keepers, the fog signals were labor-intensive. They spent hours shoveling coal and coddling the delicate settings of boilers. Electricity eventually relieved much of this work.

Along the way, myriad peculiar inventions came and went. A wave-actuated fog signal was installed at Farallon Light off San Francisco. It used the rush of waves through a blowhole to produce a burst of air that caused a locomotive whistle to scream. The device was not successful since the whistle sounded irregularly and required choppy seas to work. Fog usually rolls in when seas are calm.

Colorful comments about fog signals pepper the pages of lightkeepers' logbooks and diaries. At Point Reyes Light in California the children used the foghouse coal chute as a sliding board. A mother wrote glibly that her baby's first words were not the traditional "ma-ma" or "da-da," but a roaring "be-ooohhh!" In foggy Washington, Cape Flattery's lightkeepers learned to pause in their conversations when the signals sounded, and they often maintained the odd habit long after retirement. A few miles down the coast at Destruction Island Lighthouse, a lightkeeper's bull mistook the station's new foghorn for a rival bull and attacked it.

No matter the sound, there was always commentary. People ashore either loved or hated the lighthouse fog signals. Most considered the sounds a welcome lullaby from the sea, while a few strongly objected to the near-constant cacophony. Some didn't understand fog signaling at all. In the 1880s a Salish Indian observed government workers building a fog signal in Puget Sound, all the time wondering how it would work. When the horn roared to life, he pronounced it useless: "Horn go boo! boo! all the time, but fog come in anyway."

Point Sur Light Station
CARMEL

FOR MORE INFORMATION
Central Coast Lighthouse
Keepers
P.O. Box 223014
Carmel, CA 93922
831.649.7139
e-mail info@pointsur.org
www.pointsur.org

DIRECTIONS
Point Sur is visible from
Highway 1 about 19 miles south
of Carmel. Watch for signs for
the turnoff to the lighthouse
parking area. Visitors must hike
a steep half-mile hill to reach
the light station.

The 369-foot humpback of rock that forms Point Sur was a well-known landmark for navigators in the nineteenth century. In 1889 it became the site of a rugged granite lighthouse with a flashing first-order Fresnel lens and steam fog signal. A small-gauge railway brought supplies to the lighthouse and to its triplex keepers' dwelling.

The lens was removed when the station was automated in 1972, and it was given to the Maritime Museum of Monterey. Point Sur State Park was established at this time and included the lighthouse reservation. Today the station is open for tours courtesy of the Central Coast Lighthouse Keepers.

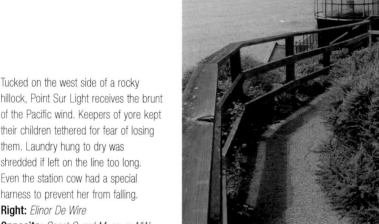

Tucked on the west side of a rocky
hillock, Point Sur Light receives the brunt
of the Pacific wind. Keepers of yore kept
their children tethered for fear of losing
them. Laundry hung to dry was
shredded if left on the line too long.
Even the station cow had a special
harness to prevent her from falling.
Right: *Elinor De Wire*
Opposite: *Coast Guard Museum NW*

Point Vicente Light Station
RANCHO PALOS VERDES

FOR MORE INFORMATION
Point Vicente Interpretive Center
31501 Palos Verdes Dr. West
Rancho Palos Verdes, CA 90275
310.541.0334
www.sanpedrochamber.com/
champint/ptviclhs.htm

HOURS OF OPERATION
The center is open the
second Saturday of every
month, 10 A.M. to 3 P.M.

DIRECTIONS
From I-405, take Hawthorne
Boulevard south to West
Palos Verdes Drive. Watch for
signs to the Point Vicente
Interpretive Center.

The 55-foot reinforced-concrete lighthouse at Point Vicente is one of California's newest sentinels, built in 1926. Its electric beacon marked the jutting Palos Verdes Peninsula and helped ships navigate southward into Los Angeles. The station had three keepers' dwellings and a fog signal. Between 1934 and 1980 the station also operated a radiobeacon.

The lighthouse was automated in 1971 but still operates its original Fresnel lens. Coast Guard personnel live on the grounds. The station can be viewed from the nearby Point Vicente Interpretive Center, which also has information on occasional special tours.

In the 1950s, Point Vicente Light's landward windows were painted white to prevent the light from shining in nearby house windows. The eerie glow spawned a delightful ghost tale. *Elinor De Wire*

Punta Gorda Lighthouse
PETROLIA

Swift currents and high winds make the Mendocino coast a dangerous place. A light station was built at Punta Gorda in 1912, about 12 miles south of Mendocino. The modest tower consisted of an iron lantern perched on a square concrete building. Three dwellings, a fog signal house, a barn, and a shed completed the station.

The lighthouse was extinguished in 1951, after only 39 years of service. It was expensive to maintain and the need for the beacon had diminished over the years. The station was transferred to the Bureau of Land Management in 1963. Only the tower and oilhouse remain standing. Neither is open for tours but the grounds may be visited.

DIRECTIONS
From Highway 1 at Petrolia, take Mattole Road to Lighthouse Road. Park at the beach and walk 3.5 miles to the lighthouse. The walk is rigorous and the beach can be impassable at high tide.

Punta Gorda Lighthouse did not have a road connecting it to civilization until 1915. Even then, no car could traverse it, and keepers used horses to travel the 11 miles to Petrolia. *Coast Guard Archives*

St. George Reef Lighthouse
CRESCENT CITY

FOR MORE INFORMATION
St. George Reef Lighthouse
Preservation Society
P.O. Box 577
Crescent City, CA 95531
707.464.8299
e-mail
tours@stgeorgereeflighthouse.us
www.stgeorgereeflighthouse.us

The most expensive lighthouse in the United States, St. George Reef Light went into service in 1892 to mark dangerous rocks 9 miles off the coast. The offshore stone tower took almost ten years to construct, at a cost of $704,000. Its first-order lens flashed red and white.

Only men were permitted to live at the remote light tower. Storms and isolation made their lives difficult. A crew of five keepers rotated duty three-months-on and two-months-off. In 1975 their work ended when a large lighted navigation buoy was anchored west of the lighthouse.

The lens was removed and put on display in the Del Norte County Historical Society Museum. The tower stood dark and forlorn for a number of years until a nonprofit group adopted it and began restoration.

On clear days the lighthouse can be seen from beaches near Crescent City. Helicopter tours are offered.

As twilight merges with slate skies over the moody Pacific Ocean, the low intensity beacon of St. George Reef sits ready for service. It is lighted only on special occasions.
Elinor De Wire

Opposite and above: The 1865 wreck of the sidewheeler *Brother Jonathan*, in which 150 people perished, convinced the Lighthouse Service to build a lighthouse on St. George Reef. It took almost 30 years to complete and ran well over budget. *Elinor De Wire*

San Luis Obispo Light Station
AVILA BEACH

FOR MORE INFORMATION
San Luis Lighthouse Keepers
P.O. Box 13556
San Luis Obispo, CA 93406
Contact the San Luis
Lighthouse Keepers for
dates of special tours.

Completed in 1890 to guide shipping into the burgeoning Port San Luis (then Port Harford), the lighthouse was a near-twin of the Victorian sentinels at Point Fermin and Point Hueneme. It had a flashing fourth-order Fresnel lens. The station was remote, dry, and windblown. A steep, rough wagon road provided access, and water was brought through a 3.5-mile pipeline from Pecho Creek.

When the station was automated with a modern optic in 1974, the classical lens was given to the San Luis Obispo Historical Museum. By this time the Pacific Gas & Electric Company's Diablo Canyon facility surrounded the station, preventing visitor access.

Restoration of the site began in 1978 and continues under the aegis of the San Luis Lighthouse Keepers.

Victorian majesty aptly describes San Luis Obispo Light. Situated near the Diablo Canyon nuclear facility, public access to it is limited. A local preservation group has done a commendable job of restoring the station. *Courtesy of Derith Bennett*

Santa Cruz Lighthouse
SANTA CRUZ

The first lighthouse at Santa Cruz was a wooden cottage-style sentinel built in 1869. It was torn down in 1948 after erosion threatened to topple it.

The current brick lighthouse was built in 1967 as a family memorial, honoring eighteen-year-old Mark Abbott, who drowned off the point while surfing. The lantern came from the defunct Oakland Harbor Lighthouse. The lighthouse is home to the Santa Cruz Surfing Museum.

FOR MORE INFORMATION
Santa Cruz Surfing Museum
701 West Cliff Drive
Santa Cruz, CA 95062
831.420.6289
www.santacruzsurfing
museum.org

HOURS OF OPERATION
Summer: Wednesday through Monday, 12 P.M. to 4 P.M.
Winter: Thursday through Monday, 12 P.M. to 4 P.M.

DIRECTIONS
From Santa Cruz Beach Boardwalk, take West Cliff Drive. The lighthouse is easy to spot and there is ample parking.

Much different in appearance and purpose than its 1869 predecessor, the modern-day Santa Cruz Lighthouse memorializes a lost surfer. It went into service in 1967. *Elinor De Wire*

Table Bluff Lighthouse
EUREKA

DIRECTIONS
From US 101 in Eureka, take SR 225 to Woodley Island. Follow signs to the marina and the lighthouse.

A guide for Humboldt Bay, the lighthouse was built in 1982 to replace an old cottage-style beacon on North Spit, which was wracked by erosion and earthquakes. The new tower was a duplicate of the Victorian sentinels at Ballast Point and Point San Luis Obispo. The North Spit light's fourth-order lens was transferred to the new tower.

The station was occupied by keepers until after World War II, when the homes were torn down and the tower was automated. The classical lens was removed and replaced by a modern aerobeacon.

In 1975 the lighthouse was discontinued. Local residents removed the top of the tower and took it to Woodley Island Marina for display. The original lens also is exhibited on Woodley Island at Humboldt Bay Maritime Museum on Second Street.

Residents of Humboldt Bay were so fond of the defunct lighthouse at Table Bluff that they removed its top portion in the 1980s and relocated it to a popular marina.
Elinor DeWire

Trinidad Head Lighthouse
TRINIDAD

In 1871 a small brick lighthouse was placed in service on a lofty headland enclosing Trinidad Bay. It closed a dark gap between Crescent City and Humboldt Bay. A handsome keeper's house stood on the hill behind the lighthouse. In 1898 a fog signal was added to the station—a 2-ton bell whose percussive bongs loosened rocks on the cliff.

In 1947 a modern optic replaced the fourth-order Fresnel lens, and a bell upstaged the horn. Both the lens and bell were put on display on the waterfront in the town of Trinidad. The keeper's house was torn down and a triplex was built for Coast Guard personnel. The station was automated in the 1970s. It is closed to the public.

DIRECTIONS
The light station can be seen in the distance from various spots along US 101 south of Trinidad. The original lens and bell, along with a replica of the lighthouse, are located at the foot of Trinity Street, on the waterfront in the town of Trinidad.

Keeper Fred L. Harrington surveys the sea from Trinidad Lighthouse. On December 31, 1913, Harrington saw a huge wave strike the cliff below the tower and send water nearly 200 feet up and over the lantern. *National Archives*

Walton Lighthouse
SANTA CRUZ

DIRECTIONS
The lighthouse is not open for tours but it can be viewed from the Santa Cruz Marina or from the adjacent beach. It can be reached on foot via a breakwater.

California's newest lighthouse was built in 2001, on the west jetty of Santa Cruz. The Walton Lighthouse (also called the Santa Cruz Harbor Light) is a steel-plate tower that shows a modern green optic 54 feet above sea level. The light was dedicated on June 9, 2002. The light received its name from one of its patrons, Charles Walton, who donated $60,000 for the project, in memory of his brother who served in the Merchant Marines.

New lighthouses are a rarity, but Walton Lighthouse in Santa Cruz is an exception. It was built in 2001 and named for a private donor.
Elinor De Wire

Yerba Buena Lighthouse
SAN FRANCISCO

Yerba Buena Island was home to the Lighthouse Service Depot when a lighthouse was built on its southeast shore in 1875. The small wooden tower exhibited a fixed fourth-order light and a nearby foghouse held a steam whistle. Above the tower was a beautiful gabled keepers' duplex. Proximity of the depot made life easier for the keepers, since supplies and repairmen were close at hand.

The island was dwarfed by the Transbay Bridge in 1936, and floodlights were added to make the lighthouse more visible to ships. Automation came in the late 1950s, though the Fresnel lens was not removed and remains in service today.

The attractive keeper's dwelling is now the home of a Coast Guard officer. The lighthouse is on government property and is not open to the public.

Yerba Buena Island, meaning "island of good herbs," lent its name to a small lighthouse in 1875. The island was isolated prior to construction of the Bay Bridge in 1936. One keeper's daughter, determined to attend school, used a sailboat to get San Francisco on weekdays. **Left:** *Courtesy of Derith Bennett* **Above:** *Elinor De Wire*

Chapter Two

Lighthouses of Oregon

FOR MORE INFORMATION:
U.S. Lighthouse Society,
Oregon Chapter
PO Box 1200
Port Orford, OR 97465
www.randomb.com

Explorers and settlers encountered fewer perils along the Oregon coast than in other parts of the Pacific. Though dotted with capes and headlands and pounded by winter storms, only one major navigational obstacle faced mariners between Northern California and the Columbia River: the critical turning point at Cape Blanco.

Surprisingly, however, this site was not the first place along the Oregon Coast to be lighted. While nine lighthouses were planned for California, and five for what would someday become the state of Washington, Congress felt Oregon needed only one lighthouse. Funds were precious in the 1850s and Oregon lacked the large ports of California and the major waterways of Washington. It was therefore left out of the lighthouse boom.

The site chosen for Oregon's first lighthouse was the Umpqua River, named for the natives of the coast. A burgeoning lumber trade and discovery of gold in southwest Oregon Territory spurred the growth of a settlement at the river mouth. The lighthouse was constructed in 1857 but it lasted only four years. In the spring of 1861, a heavy snowpack in the mountains melted and flooded the Umpqua River, washing away the lighthouse. It was not rebuilt until 1894, as funds were lacking and the construction of other lighthouses took priority.

Strapped for funding due to the Civil War, Congress did little to improve West Coast lighthouses in general until after 1865. In 1866 Cape Arago Light was built on an islet off the entrance to the busy lumber port of Coos Bay. In 1870, Cape Blanco, the most dangerous headland along the coast and the major reckoning point for ships, was finally lighted. The dramatic sea-swept sentinel on Tillamook Rock, on a stump of basalt one mile off Cannon Beach, flashed on in 1881 as an aid to ships headed in and out of the Columbia River. It quickly earned a reputation as the worst place to work on the West Coast.

In 1894, the same year the Umpqua River Lighthouse was rebuilt, Heceta Head Light went into service and was immediately dubbed the most beautiful lighthouse on the West Coast. Six more Oregon lighthouses were in operation by 1900.

The first lighthouse at Coos Bay was an iron tower on stilts, built in 1866. No roads led to the site, so the first keeper, his wife, and baby took a boat down the bay and then rode pack horses through thick forest to the cape. *Coast Guard Museum NW*

As Oregon moved into the twentieth century, lighthouse construction slowed. Desdemona Sands Light, built in 1902 on a mudflat in the Columbia River, was the last sentinel built in the state. Discontinued in 1934, it washed away piece by piece as the river reshaped its course. The fabulous Fresnel lens from the lighthouse ended up in a private home. It was later found by a historian from Mukilteo, Washington, and placed on display in Mukilteo Lighthouse.

By the late 1980s all Oregon lighthouses had been automated. Slowly, groups formed to care for them. Seven of the sentinels are now open to the public. The Oregon chapter of the U.S. Lighthouse Society provides information on the state's lighthouses. Visit their website at www.randomb.com or write them at P.O. Box 1200, Port Orford, OR 97465.

Cape Blanco marks a critical navigational turning point on the West Coast, yet it was not the first place to receive a lighthouse in Oregon. A sentinel was not built here until 1870.
Elinor De Wire

Cape Arago Lighthouse
Coos Bay

The busy port of Coos Bay got its first lighthouse in 1866. It was an octagonal iron tower perched on a platform supported by stilts. The lantern exhibited a fourth-order Fresnel lens. The lighthouse stood on an islet a few hundred feet offshore at Cape Arago and was accessed by boat. In 1891 a wooden bridge was built to connect the islet to the mainland, and a fog trumpet was added to the station.

DIRECTIONS
The lighthouse is located on tribal land and is not open to the public. It is visible from a turnout in Cape Arago State Park.

Erosion prompted the construction of a new lighthouse in 1909. It lasted until 1934, when erosion again damaged the tower beyond repair. The third and current concrete sentinel remains in service but was automated in 1966. Its classical Fresnel lens was removed in 1993 and replaced by a plastic aerobeacon. The lens is now displayed at the Coast Guard Air Station in North Bend.

Erosion has plagued weatherworn Cape Arago Lighthouse since its inception. Three lighthouses have stood on the cape, including the current tower, built in 1934. *Dean Carter*

Cape Blanco Light Station
PORT OXFORD

FOR MORE INFORMATION
Friends of Cape Blanco
P.O. Box 1178
Port Orford, OR 97465
541.332.0248
www.hugheshouse.org

HOURS OF OPERATION
April 1 through October 31,
Tuesday through Sunday,
10 A.M. to 3:30 P.M.

DIRECTIONS
From US 101 north of Port
Orford, drive west on Cape
Blanco Highway for about
5 miles.

The lighthouse was built in 1870 on a prominent windy point where ships make a critical turn along the coast. The brick tower is 59 feet tall and shines from a 200-foot bluff. It is the oldest original lighthouse in Oregon, its first-order Fresnel lens still operates. The lighthouse was automated in the 1980s, when it became part of Cape Blanco State Park. It was refurbished by the Bureau of Land Management in 2003.

The Cape Blanco Lighthouse received a much-needed facelift in 2003.
Elinor De Wire

An antique postcard proclaims Cape Blanco's distinction of being the westernmost point on the Oregon coast. In its heyday, the station was an oasis in the wilderness with only one rough, cliff-top road for access. *Coast Guard Museum NW*

Cape Meares Lighthouse
TILLAMOOK

FOR MORE INFORMATION
Friends of Cape Meares
Lighthouse
P.O. Box 262
Oceanside, OR 97134
Call 503.842.2244 to schedule
a tour.
e-mail Avalon@harborside.com
www.capemeareslighthouse.org

HOURS OF OPERATION
Open daily from April through
October, 11 A.M. to 4 P.M.
The last tour of the day departs
at 3:15 P.M.

DIRECTIONS
From US 101 near Tillamook,
follow signs for Cape Meares
State Park and the lighthouse.
A broad trail leads down from
the parking area to the
lighthouse and a gift shop.

The stocky, iron tower at Cape Meares went into service in 1890 on a precipitous cliff overlooking Three Arches. Keepers' dwellings sat far up the hill behind the lighthouse. There was no road into the town of Tillamook until 1894.

In 1963 the first-order lens was shut down and an automatic modern optic, mounted on top of a square concrete building beside the tower, took its place. The lighthouse was scheduled for demolition, but public protest resulted in its transfer to Tillamook County and Oregon State Parks.

Red panels on the first-order lens of Cape Meares Lighthouse add beauty but also function, distinguishing the beacon from its sister sentries. The lens was recently refurbished and returned to the lantern as part of a large-scale restoration of the station. *Jessica De Wire*

Stubby Cape Meares Light had few steps to the top but a huge optic occupied its lantern. The lens had to be covered in the daytime to protect it from dust and sunlight. The original workroom shows in this picture from about 1900. *Coast Guard Museum NW*

Coquille River Lighthouse
BANDON

FOR MORE INFORMATION
www.rudyalicelighthouse.net/
NWLts/Coquille/Coquille.htm

HOURS OF OPERATION
Wednesday through Sunday,
11 A.M. to 3 P.M.

DIRECTIONS
From the west side of Highway
101 north of Bandon, enter
Bullards Beach State Park and
follow signs to the lighthouse.

Guarding the north jetty of the Coquille River, the lighthouse has stood watch since 1896. The 40-foot stone tower is connected to a foghouse and sits amidst sea oats sand dunes. It held a fourth-order Fresnel lens that served until 1939, when the Coast Guard installed an automatic light at the end of the jetty. The decommissioned lighthouse was vandalized repeatedly and deteriorated until 1976, when Oregon State Parks adopted it. The state restored and relighted Coquille River Lighthouse in 1991 as a private navigational aid.

The High Victorian Italianate sentinel at Bandon has a short tower and spacious attached foghouse. From 1896 to 1939, coal-fueled steam pipes produced distinctive sound warnings. *Elinor De Wire*

Heceta Head Lighthouse
YACHATS

The 56-foot lighthouse stands on a magnificent headland north of Florence and has served ships since 1894. It operates a first-order lens and shines from 205 feet above sea level. The light was electrified in 1934 and automated in 1963. The station then became part of the Siuslaw National Forest. Only one of the two Queen Anne–style keepers' residences remains, and it has been converted to a bed and breakfast. A small interpretive center is located in the old garage.

FOR MORE INFORMATION
Heceta Head B&B
92072 Hwy 101 South
Yachats, OR 97498
toll-free 866.547.3696
www.hecetalighthouse.com

HOURS OF OPERATION
Daily, 12 P.M. to 5 P.M.

DIRECTIONS
From Highway 101 eleven miles north of Florence, turn west into the parking area at Devils Elbow State Park and follow the marked trail to the light station.

Opposite: Often cited as the West Coast's most beautiful lighthouse, Heceta Head Light stands on a high bluff near Devils Elbow State Park. One of the original keepers' homes has been converted to a stylish B&B. **Above:** *Elinor De Wire Collection* **Right:** *Elinor De Wire*

Tillamook Rock Lighthouse
CANNON BEACH

Nicknamed "Terrible Tilly" by lightkeepers of the past who dreaded duty on the isolated 1881 sentinel, Tillamook Rock is the only offshore lighthouse in Oregon. Built to aid northbound ships headed for the Columbia River, the tower's first-order Fresnel lens shone from 133 feet above the sea. Five keepers were

DIRECTIONS
The lighthouse is visible from Ecola State Park, off Highway 101 just north of Cannon Beach.

assigned to the lonely lighthouse. Their families lived ashore, since the site was too dangerous for women and children.

In 1957 the light was discontinued and its duties were transferred to a large buoy. The tower stood dark and empty until the 1980s, when it was purchased by a real estate company and opened as the Eternity at Sea Columbarium. It is not open to the public.

A forlorn haunt of seabirds and often pummeled by Pacific storms, Tillamook Rock Lighthouse was considered a difficult assignment. Only men served on the light.
Right: *Elinor De Wire Collection*

Opposite: *Jessica De Wire*

Umpqua River Light Station
REEDSPORT

HOURS OF OPERATION
Wednesday through Saturday,
10 A.M. to 5 P.M. and Sunday,
1 P.M. to 5 P.M.

DIRECTIONS
From Highway 101 six miles
south of Reedsport, turn west
into Umpqua State Park and
follow signs to the lighthouse.

Established in 1857, this first lighthouse in Oregon went into service at the entrance to the Umpqua River, where it aided vessels carrying passengers and supplies to gold fields in the state's interior. The cottage-style sentinel, with a 92-foot tower rising from its roof, lasted only a few years before river floods ruined it.

The second and current lighthouse was built at a higher elevation. Lighted in 1894, the 65-foot tower is crowned by an opulent ruby-paneled Fresnel lens. There is a museum and gift shop near the lighthouse.

Oregon's first lighthouse went into operation at Umpqua River but soon succumbed to floods. Its replacement, built in 1894 at higher elevation, has withstood the elements. Its magnificent ruby glass lens (right) stands 10 feet tall and still serves ships. **Opposite:** *Coast Guard Museum NW* **Right and below:** *Elinor De Wire*

Things That Go Bump in the Night

Every lighthouse has a ghost tale to tell; some have several. By its very nature, a lighthouse is truly a scary place, especially at night. Waves crash about its walls, winds sigh through the interior, shipwrecks lie at its feet, and shadows and echoes spawn sinister thoughts.

West Coast maritime historian James Gibbs tells a wonderful yarn about a Puget Sound lightkeeper and his wife who had an experience with the supernatural. The name of their lighthouse has been lost in the telling and retelling of the tale, which is probably for the best. Who, other than ghost-chasers, would visit a lighthouse where doors open and close on their own and spirits reside?

The couple sat quietly reading one windy evening. Their cat lay curled asleep by the stove, deep in feline dreams. Suddenly it rose up and arched its back, eyes wide. The lightkeeper and his wife heard footsteps clomping down the stairs from the light tower above. The cat hissed and backed away, as its eyes followed some invisible presence moving across the room. Unseen hands opened the front door, and the wind howled through, ruffling the pages of the couple's books. A moment later, the ghost exited into the night, slamming the door behind it. Had some spirit escaped lighthouse purgatory? The keeper and his wife exchanged curious expressions, then resumed their reading. The cat returned to her nap.

Such stories pepper the pages of lighthouse diaries and circulate among descendents. Sooner or later every keeper's imagination got the best of him and a ghost popped up. Over time the stories were embroidered with delicious details to make them more believable and fun. These tales are part of the fabric of lighthouse lore, reminders of the moments of loneliness and boredom of life in a lighthouse.

At Heceta Head Lighthouse, the restless spirit of a woman walks the grounds. It's said her child died at the station in the 1890s and she was not told the location of the grave, lest she grieve all the more. The Gray Lady, named for her silver hair and wrinkled visage, still searches for her lost baby. She's been seen in the attic and often lurks in one particular bedroom. A similar wraith wanders the path behind Yaquina Bay Lighthouse, though this ghost is a teenage girl who supposedly disappeared at the sentinel after it was abandoned in 1874 and had become the hangout of local youths.

At Battery Point Lighthouse off Crescent City, California, lightkeepers referred to the ghosts as their "misty friends." A rocking chair sometimes rocked by itself and things moved around mysteriously. Unseen hands touched visitors. One day an oil-lamp globe inexplicably leaped off its perch and hurled itself to the floor. At this same station in the nineteenth century, a lightkeeper was "taken away" because he told government inspectors that little mermaids came to visit him on the rocks surrounding the lighthouse.

Whether we believe in lighthouse ghosts or simply chalk them up to fertile imaginations or the innocent pranks of bored keepers, their stories exist and will be told over and over for years to come. Sometimes ghost tales outshine the true history of the lighthouses. But in a sense, the stories are much a part of history. We can doubt their veracity, but not their source.

Visit a lighthouse some dark, stormy night when the seas are raging and winds pummel the lantern. See for yourself just what stimulates the imagination.

Yaquina Bay Lighthouse
NEWPORT

A wooden cottage-style lighthouse was built on a hill overlooking Yaquina Bay in 1871. It served the burgeoning lumber and oyster trade of central Oregon. Only four years into its career, the lighthouse was decommissioned when a taller lighthouse replaced it on Yaquina Head. Its fifth-order Fresnel lens was put in storage.

Various tenants, including the U.S. Army and U.S. Lifesaving Service, occupied the lighthouse over the next century. In 1974 restoration began under the aegis of the Oregon Historical Society. Today the lighthouse is a museum.

FOR MORE INFORMATION
Yaquina Lights
P.O. Box 410
Newport, OR 97365
541.574.3100
www.yaquinalights.org

HOURS OF OPERATION
Memorial Day through the end of September,
11 A.M. to 5 P.M.
Off-season, 12 P.M. to 4 P.M.

DIRECTIONS
From Highway 101 in Newport, follow signs for Yaquina Bay State Park and Historic Lighthouse. The lighthouse is located at the west end of Elisabeth Street.

Though it served only four years, Yaquina Bay Lighthouse has been used for other purposes, including a U.S. Lifesaving Station from 1906 until 1934. *Newport Historical Society*

Yaquina Head Lighthouse
NEWPORT

FOR MORE INFORMATION
See Yaquina Lights under
Yaquina Bay Lighthouse.

HOURS OF OPERATION
June through Labor Day:
daily, 9 A.M. to 4 P.M.
Day after Labor Day through
October 31: weekdays,
12 P.M. to 4 P.M. (self-guided
tours); weekends, 9 A.M. to
11:30 A.M. (ranger-led tours)
and 12 P.M. to 4 P.M.
(self-guided tours) November
1 through May: 12 P.M. to 4
P.M. (self-guided tours only)

DIRECTIONS
From Highway 101 three miles
north of Newport, turn west at
the sign for the lighthouse.

Oregon's tallest lighthouse, this stately 1874 sentinel on Yaquina Head rises 93 feet high, and its first-order Fresnel lens casts a beam more than 20 miles out to sea on clear nights. Three keepers resided in a single large dwelling until 1939, when the Coast Guard razed the old house and built new quarters. The station was automated in the 1980s and all but the tower and workroom were torn down.

The site was transferred to the Bureau of Land Management in 1993. Today it is completely restored and includes a spacious visitor center.

A majestic spire, Yaquina Head Lighthouse contains 370,000 bricks and rises 114 steps up a spiral staircase to the ornate iron lantern. Its first order lens was shipped in pieces from France to New York City, then on to Panama where it was hauled by wagon to the Pacific Ocean. Another ship finished the journey to Newport.
Above: *Elinor De Wire* **Opposite:** *Jessica DeWire*

Chapter Three

Lighthouses of Washington

No lighthouse greeted Captain George Vancouver in 1792 as his ships explored the foggy coast of present-day Washington, nor did a beacon guide Lewis and Clark on their 1804 landmark journey to the mouth of the Columbia River. A half-century would pass before Washington became a territory of the United States and pioneers began arriving to fish, cut timber, and homestead. With only crude trails providing access to settlements, and the Cascade Mountains posing a forbidding obstacle to travelers, Washington's waterways became its highways. Plans were made to tame its wild shores with lighthouses.

The first official navigational light went into service at Cape Disappointment in 1856 to mark the Columbia River Bar, one of the world's most daunting shipping obstacles. Lights also went into service at Willapa Bay—a busy oyster and lumber port—and at Cape Flattery, Dungeness Spit, and Smith Island in the Strait of Juan de Fuca. By the 1880s the inside waters of Puget Sound had been marked from Point No Point south to Olympia. After Washington became a state in 1889, the dangerous islands of the San Juan archipelago also received lights.

With the exception of the brick tower at Cape Disappointment, Washington's early sentinels were fashioned after the Cape Cod–style lighthouses of California. The towers rose from simple dwellings. Fogbells or stream signals sounded warnings through the frequent mists. Toward the end of the nineteenth century and up until about 1920, Astoria architect Carl Leick was the dean of lighthouse construction throughout the Pacific Northwest. His designs usually incorporated a tower and foghouse in a brick or concrete structure coated in parge, a stucco-like mixture that provided protection in the wet climate.

Twenty-six lighthouses and three lightships were established in Washington between 1856 and 1914. Many were rebuilt after the elements caused them to deteriorate or the shorelines changed. Several, including the lights at Willapa Bay, Ediz Hook, and Slip Point, washed away and were replaced by steel skeleton towers. Twenty traditional lighthouses still stand in the Evergreen State, all operational except for Admiralty Head Lighthouse.

Washington's lightkeepers came largely from local communities and brought their families to the stations. The keeper with the longest tenure was John Cowan, who served at Cape Flattery Lighthouse from 1900 to 1932. He had previously served at two Oregon lighthouses. Several women also held

Lime Kiln Light's cold waters and rich salmon run draws pods of orcas in summer. A whale study is housed inside the tower. *Elinor De Wire*

lightkeeping jobs, including Mabel Bretherton of North Head Lighthouse and sisters Georgia and Flora Pearson at Red Bluff Lighthouse.

The Coast Guard, which took control of navigational aids in 1939, began modernizing and automating the lighthouses and fog signals in Washington. The last station to be manned was West Point Light in Seattle, which was automated in 1985. Coast Guard keeper Marvin Gerbers doused the lighthouse with champagne to bid farewell to the lightkeeping era and usher in self-sufficiency.

Following automation, many of the state's lighthouses

Cape Flattery Light guards Tatoosh Island, which was used by the Makah for potlatches and fishing operations long ago. Besides the lighthouse and fog signal, it had a weather station and radio compass station. *Elinor De Wire*

were leased or transferred to municipal and nonprofit groups. Ten lighthouses and one lightship are open to the public as museums, overnight rentals, or attractions in parks. The Washington Lightkeepers Association provides information on the state's lighthouses and lightships. Visit their website at www.walightkeepers.com. Write to the group at P.O. Box 984, Seabeck, WA 98380.

The patriarch of Cape Flattery's lightkeepers was John Cowan, who served as principle keeper of the light from 1900 until 1932. His wife and nine children lived ashore during the school year but joined him on the island in the summer. *Seattle Museum of History & Industry*

Admiralty Head Lighthouse
COUPEVILLE

Built in 1861 on the southwest shore of Whidbey Island, the lighthouse was originally called Red Bluff Light. It was a wooden house with a lantern rising from its roof that displayed a fourth-order Fresnel lens. The lighthouse was rebuilt in 1903 north of the bluff on Fort Casey. A spacious two-story residence was attached to the brick tower. In 1922 Admiralty Head was discontinued due to changes in the shipping lanes.

Five years later the lens and lantern were removed and transferred to New Dungeness Lighthouse. The fort closed after World War II, and the grounds and lighthouse became state park property. The lighthouse later was restored and opened to the public. It is not an active aid to mariners.

FOR MORE INFORMATION
Keepers of Admiralty Head
Lighthouse
P.O. Box 5000
Coupeville, WA 98239
360.679.7391
www.admiraltyhead.wsu.edu

DIRECTIONS
On Whidbey Island, turn left onto Fort Casey Road a half-mile north of the Keystone Ferry Dock and proceed into Fort Casey State Park. Follow signs for the lighthouse.

Because of its unique style and beauty, Admiralty Head Lighthouse was chosen in 1989 for a series of stamps depicting lighthouses. Inactive since 1922, it is a museum within Fort Casey State Park. *Elinor De Wire*

Alki Point Light Station
West Seattle

HOURS OF OPERATION
Local Coast Guard Flotilla
volunteers open the
lighthouse for tours on
weekends, Memorial Day
through Labor Day, 12 P.M.
to 3 P.M.. No tours are given
Fourth of July weekend.

DIRECTIONS
From I-5, take exit 163 onto
the West Seattle Freeway. At
SW Admiral Way, turn right,
then take another right onto
63rd Avenue. Turn right again
on Alki Avenue and drive to
the lighthouse.

In 1868, 17 years after the first Seattle pioneers landed on Alki Beach, a crude lantern served as a light for ships. In 1887 it was improved with the construction of a wooden scaffold that exhibited a lens-lantern, which operated until 1913, when an integrated light tower and foghouse was built.

The 37-foot tower had a fourth-order Fresnel lens. Fog trumpets blared from the foghouse below the tower. Behind the lighthouse were two comfortable dwellings for the keepers. In the 1960s the lens was removed and a modern optic was installed. It was automated in 1984.

The original Fresnel lens from Alki Point Light is on display at Admiralty Head Lighthouse. The old lens-lantern is on exhibit at the Coast Guard Museum Northwest located in Seattle.

Situated on the southern shore of Seattle's Elliott Bay, little Alki Light is well known to ferry travelers. Its keepers' quarters are homes for senior officers in the 13th Coast Guard District.
Elinor De Wire

Browns Point Light Station
BROWNS POINT

A lens-lantern hoisted atop a wooden post served as the first beacon for the Port of Tacoma. It was lighted in 1887 on Point Brown, at the eastern entrance to Commencement Bay. In 1903 the lens-lantern was moved to a two-story wooden tower, which also housed a fogbell. A keeper's house was built behind the tower.

The station was electrified in 1922, the same year it became known as Browns Point. Eleven years later, the wooden lighthouse burned down and was replaced by a reinforced-concrete tower with a modern optic. It was automated in 1963. In 1998 the Points NE Historical Society restored the keeper's dwelling and opened it as a vacation rental in which renters have the opportunity to become "light keepers" for a week, conducting tours and performing light chores as they enjoy their rental.

FOR INFORMATION ON THE RENTAL
Points NE Historical Society
1000 Town Center, Suite 180,
PMB 135
Browns Point, WA 98422
253.927.2536
www.pointsnortheast.org

HOURS OF OPERATION
The lighthouse is closed but grounds are open daily during daylight hours as part of Tacoma's Metropolitan Parks District.

DIRECTIONS
From I-5, take exit 137 and go north to the exit for state road 509 (Marine View Drive). Drive about 5 miles to a small shopping village, and look for a sign for Browns Point. Turn left and follow this road to the lighthouse.

Browns Point Light at Tacoma has an intriguing history. Its first keeper, Oscar Brown, was an accomplished musician who offered music lessons. Builders constructed a special alcove in the dwelling's parlor for Brown's piano.
U.S. Lighthouse Society

Burrows Island Lighthouse
ANACORTES

FOR INFORMATION ON BOAT TOURS
Northwest Schooner Society
P.O. Box 9504
Seattle, WA 98109
800.551.NWSS
www.nwschooner.org

Burrows Island, a small island facing Rosario Strait, has had a lighthouse since 1906. The integrated 34-foot wooden tower and foghouse exhibited a fourth-order Fresnel lens with red sectors to warn of shoals to the south. A fog trumpet blared seaward from the west side of the foghouse. Steep cliffs around the site required construction of a boathouse with a derrick. A large, two-story dwelling for the keeper stood behind the lighthouse.

The station was automated in 1972. The Fresnel lens was removed in 1997 in favor of a modern optic. The lighthouse is closed and the site is not open to visitors, but it can be viewed by boat.

The tidy lighthouse on Burrows Island was dwarfed by a large keeper's house. The Coast Guard later added a second house, shown in a 1950s photo (top). Since automation in 1972, the station has been frequently vandalized. With windows sealed and doors padlocked, it awaits transfer to a worthy public group that will care for it. **Above:** *U.S. Coast Guard* **Opposite:** *Elinor De Wire*

Cape Disappointment Lighthouse
ILWACO

FOR MORE INFORMATION
Washington Parks &
Recreational Commission,
Long Beach Area
P.O. Box 488
Ilwaco, WA 98624
360.642.3078
www.parks.wa.gov

HOURS OF OPERATION
The lighthouse is closed to
visitors but the grounds are
open during daylight hours.

DIRECTIONS
From US 101 at Ilwaco, follow
signs south to Fort Canby State
Park. View the lighthouse from
the Lewis & Clark Interpretive
Center, or park in the Coast
Guard visitor lot and walk up
the steep hill to the tower.

The oldest lighthouse in Washington, Cape Disappointment has marked the mouth of the Columbia River since 1856. The 53-foot brick tower stood on a lofty bluff overlooking the treacherous river bar where many shipwrecks occurred. It exhibited a first-order Fresnel lens. A fogbell was mounted in a frame building in front of the tower. About a quarter-mile back from the cliff was a keeper's dwelling.

Fort Canby was built on the cape during the Civil War and cannons were set up around the lighthouse. By 1871, percussion from cannon fire had destroyed the fogbell building and the fog signal was discontinued. In 1898 the first-order lens was transferred to nearby North Head Lighthouse and replaced by a fourth-order lens. The old dwelling is gone, replaced by a modern Coast Guard rescue-training facility.

Though the lighthouse is closed to visitors, state park rangers plan to open the lighthouse for tours in the future. Exhibits, including the first-order lens, are on display at nearby Lewis & Clark Interpretive Center.

Above: The little sentinel at Cape Disappointment had a rough beginning. Materials for the tower went to the bottom of the Columbia River in 1853 when the supply ship *Oriole* wrecked on the bar. During the Civil War, cannons were set up but never fired. *Coast Guard Archives*

Left: Cape Disappointment Lighthouse casts a red light to warn boaters of the treacherous Columbia River entrance. The sentinel is part of a large Coast Guard complex that includes a lifeboat station and surfman's school. *Elinor De Wire*

Far left: A fixed first-order lens served at Cape Disappointment from 1856 until 1898, when it was transferred to the new North Head Lighthouse. The lens is now on exhibit in the Lewis & Clark Interpretive Center. *Elinor De Wire*

Cape Flattery Light Station
NEAH BAY

DIRECTIONS
The island is off-limits to the public. A viewpoint can be accessed via a trail from a parking area 8 miles west of Neah Bay, off SR 112.

Established in 1857 on Tatoosh Island at the northwest tip of Washington state, the 65-foot brick lighthouse marks the entrance to the Strait of Juan de Fuca. It originally exhibited a first-order lens. A fogbell house and a spacious two-story dwelling were also built.

A steam fog signal later replaced the bell. A weather station was added to the site in 1883, and the Navy installed a Radio Compass Station in the 1920s. A few years later the first-order lens was replaced by a fourth-order optic. A small community of about 30 people lived on the island in the 1940s, but everyone was gone by 1977, when the station was automated with a modern, self-sufficient optic.

The lighthouse remains active. It sits on tribal land and is part of a national marine sanctuary.

A small, modern optic seems dwarfed by the lantern of Cape Flattery Lighthouse. Originally, the tower had an expensive first-order French lens. Around 1940 the lens was removed and sold to a Seattle glass company. *Elinor De Wire*

Cattle Point Lighthouse
Friday Harbor

The 35-foot lighthouse, located on the southern tip of San Juan Island, was built in 1935 to replace a lens-lantern on a pole that had been in service since 1888. In 1924 a radiobeacon was installed near the pole light and Navy personnel were assigned to the site. In addition to operating the radiobeacon, they began tending the light.

Within a decade the radiobeacon had been discontinued and the present concrete lighthouse was built. During automation in the 1960s, the top of the tower was removed. A faux lantern was installed in the 1990s for a movie production, but it has since been removed.

DIRECTIONS
The lighthouse is not open but the grounds are accessible. From Friday Harbor, take Cattle Point Road to San Juan Island Historic Site. A short trail leads from the parking area to the lighthouse.

Cattle Point Light marks a grassy knoll where British livestock grazed in the 1850s. Years later, following the famous Pig War, the site became part of the United States.
Elinor De Wire

Destruction Island Lighthouse
QUEETS

FOR MORE INFORMATION
See Grays Harbor Lighthouse

DIRECTIONS
The lighthouse is part of a marine sanctuary and is not accessible to the public. It can be viewed from several pullouts along Highway 101 near Ruby Beach.

Known to local residents as "DI," the 94-foot lighthouse was built in 1891 on a precipitous island 3 miles from shore. It exhibited a first-order Fresnel lens and operated a steam fog signal. The isolated island challenged its keepers. Storms and difficulty landing supplies made the station one of the first in Washington to be de-staffed.

When it was automated in the 1960s, most of the station buildings were razed. In 1995 the opulent Fresnel lens was dismantled and replaced by a modern solar optic. The lens was moved to Westport Maritime Museum for display.

Early lightkeepers on Destruction Island kept livestock. When the station received a new foghorn in the late 1890s, the keeper's bull mistook it for a rival and went on a rampage. Eventually, the beast grew accustomed to the bellowing horn.
Courtesy of Derith Bennett

Like a ballroom chandelier, the prisms and bull's eyes of the first-order Destruction Island lens shimmer over the walls of an exhibit hall at Westport Maritime Museum. The lens was moved from the lighthouse to the museum to protect it from vandalism. *Elinor De Wire*

Dofflemyer Point Lighthouse
LITTLE BOSTON

In 1887 a wharf post-light was set up on the northeast side of Budd Inlet, leading into the port of Olympia. In 1934 the light was upgraded and placed on a 34-foot concrete tower with a tiny iron lantern on top. An electric air horn was added as a fog signal.

The light was automated in the 1960s with a plastic optic, and the small lantern was removed. The horn was manually operated for another 20 years before it too was made self-sufficient. Both the light and fog signal remain active.

> **DIRECTIONS**
> The light sits on a private beach and is not open to the public. It can be seen from the boat ramp and marina in the small community of Boston Harbor.

Deep in the heart of Puget Sound, Dofflemyer Point Light guides shipping into the capital at Olympia. From 1965 until the 1980s, the light and fog signal were manually operated by a contract lamplighter named Madeline Campbell. *Courtesy of Pam McHugh, Boston Harbor Marina*

Elinor De Wire

Grays Harbor Lighthouse
WESTPORT

DIRECTIONS
From SR 105 in Westport, turn left on Ocean Avenue and drive about a half-mile to the viewing platform on the right. Tours of the lighthouse are available from Westport Maritime Museum on Westhaven Drive in Westport.

The tallest lighthouse in Washington, Grays Harbor was built in 1898 to guide vessels to the big lumber operations at Aberdeen and Hoquiam. The brick tower was 107 feet tall and wore a daymark of white and green. Its unusual Fresnel lens combined a set of third-order panels and a half clamshell. The site also included two dwellings and a windmill to provide water for the steam fog signal. The dwellings and foghouse were removed by the late 1960s, when the lighthouse was automated.

In 1998 the Westport-South Beach Historical Society leased the lighthouse for public tours. It was formally conveyed to the society in 2004.

Like a chambered nautilus, the stairway of Grays Harbor Lighthouse seems to spiral into oblivion. It was manufactured in San Francisco in 1897 and installed in the tower the following year. *Elinor De Wire*

Washington's tallest lighthouse at Grays Harbor has a unique third-order lens with a half clamshell. Nineteenth century engineers called it a "Lightning Light." *Elinor De Wire*

Lime Kiln Lighthouse
FRIDAY HARBOR

Established on the west side of San Juan Island in 1914 as a pole light on a bluff, this small beacon guided ships through Haro Strait. A concrete light tower and attached foghouse replaced the pole light in 1919. The new lantern showed a fourth-order Fresnel lens. Two keepers' dwellings were built on the hill behind the lighthouse. The light was an incandescent oil vapor lamp until 1940, when electric power finally reached the site. Automation came to the station in 1962.

Today the lighthouse is used for marine mammal research and includes a public whale-watching area.

FOR MORE INFORMATION
Lime Kiln State Park
1567 West Side Road
Friday Harbor, WA 98250
360.378.2044

HOURS OF OPERATION
Park rangers open the lighthouse for tours Memorial Day through Labor Day on Thursday, Friday, and Saturday evenings, 7 P.M. until sunset. The grounds are open throughout the year during regular park hours, from sunrise to sunset.

DIRECTIONS
The lighthouse is located in Lime Kiln State Park, off Westside Highway, 12 miles west of Friday Harbor.

Diagonal window frames called astragals add beauty to the lantern of Lime Kiln Light but also have a function: rain and snow easily slide off the concave panes.
Elinor De Wire

Mukilteo Light Station
MUKILTEO

FOR INFORMATION ON TOURS
Mukilteo Historical Society
304 Lincoln Avenue
Mukilteo, WA 98275
425.513.9602
e-mail
info@mukilteohistorical.org
www.mukilteohistorical.org

HOURS OF OPERATION
The station is open for tours
on weekends from April
through Labor Day,
12 P.M. to 4 P.M.

DIRECTIONS
From I-5, take the Mukilteo
Expressway exit 189 into
Mukilteo. Turn left at the ferry
dock and drive a half-block to
the lighthouse.

Built in 1906 on Elliot Point overlooking Possession Sound, the small wooden light tower and attached foghouse helped ships make a critical turn en route to the large port at Everett. The lighthouse stood 38 feet tall and exhibited a fourth-order Fresnel lens. Machinery for a fog trumpet was located on the ground floor. Two handsome keepers' dwellings flanked the lighthouse, and a windmill provided water for the homes and fog signal.

The station was electrified in 1927 when the lens was changed to a third-order. It was automated in 1990. Shortly afterward, the station was given to the city of Mukilteo and opened for tours.

All dressed up for the holidays, Mukilteo Lighthouse draws thousands of visitors every December.
Jonathan De Wire

New Dungeness Light Station
SEQUIM

Constructed in 1857, the lighthouse was a 92-foot tower incorporated into a keeper's cottage. It stood on Dungeness Spit, a 5-mile finger of sand created by the Dungeness River. The tower exhibited a third-order Fresnel lens, and a fogbell guided ships in times of low visibility. The bell later was replaced by a steam signal. A second dwelling was built in 1904.

Due to earthquake and water damage, 30 feet of the tower's upper brickwork was removed in 1927. The lantern from defunct Admiralty Head Lighthouse was brought to the spit and installed, along with a fourth-order lens. The station was automated in 1994 with a modern optic and fog signal, but a local group began staffing it to prevent vandalism and deterioration. The lens is now on display in the Coast Guard Museum Northwest in Seattle, and the fog signal has been removed. The New Dungeness Light Station Association continues to maintain the site. Members serve one-week stints as keepers.

FOR INFORMATION ON THE KEEPER PROGRAM
The New Dungeness Light Station Association
P.O. Box 1283
Sequim, WA 98382
360.683.9166
e-mail
lightkeepers@newdungeness-lighthouse.com
www.newdungenesslighthouse.com

HOURS OF OPERATION
Tours of the lighthouse are available daily, 10 A.M. to 4 P.M.

DIRECTIONS
From US 101 in Sequim, turn right on Kitchen Dick Road and follow signs for New Dungeness National Wildlife Refuge. Park at the refuge entrance and hike to the lighthouse. The hike is 11 miles roundtrip. Water and a restroom are available at the lighthouse.

Hikers enjoy a picnic on the lawn of New Dungeness Light Station after traversing the 5.5-mile sandspit to the site. The station is staffed 365 days a year by members of the New Dungeness Light Station Association. *Elinor De Wire*

North Head Light Station
ILWACO

FOR MORE INFORMATION
Cape Disappointment
State Park
P.O. Box 488
Ilwaco, WA 98624
360.642.3078
www.parks.wa.gov

DIRECTIONS
From Ilwaco, follow signs
to Fort Canby State Park.
Turn right at the sign for the
lighthouse. There is about
a quarter-mile hike to
the lighthouse.

The Spanish-style 65-foot brick lighthouse was built in 1898 on a high, windy cape overlooking the northern entrance to the Columbia River. It worked in tandem with Cape Disappointment Light to help vessels safely enter the treacherous river bar. Two spacious keepers' dwellings stood on the hill behind the tower.

The first-order lens served until 1935 when electricity was installed. A fourth-order lens was exhibited until the 1950s, when two rotating aerobeacons took over. The station was automated in 1961, and an auxiliary light on the lantern gallery later became the beacon.

The lighthouse is part of a state park and is open to the public. The dwellings are vacation rentals.

The tower at North Head stands watch over one of the nation's windiest spots. In a 1921 storm, winds were clocked at more than 100 miles per hour. Spacious homes for the keepers were protected on a forested hill behind the lighthouse. *Elinor De Wire*

Patos Island Lighthouse
BELLINGHAM

Located on the western tip of Patos Island, the lighthouse guides ships through Boundary Pass, the portal between Haro Strait and the Strait of Georgia. The incorporated tower and foghouse were built in 1908, replacing an earlier sentinel. The spacious Victorian house was razed in 1970 and replaced by modern Coast Guard quarters. The 38-foot lighthouse had a fourth-order lens until it was automated in 1974. The lens is now privately owned. The Bureau of Land Management recently acquired the site and plans to restore the buildings and open the site for tours.

DIRECTIONS
The lighthouse is accessible only by boat. Charters are available from Deer Harbor on Orcas Island and Friday Harbor on San Juan Island.

Patos Island was a remote outpost for lightkeepers of the past. Edward and Estelle Durgan raised 13 children here in the early 1900s. During a smallpox outbreak, a doctor was delayed by weather and three children died. *National Archives*

Point No Point Lighthouse

HANSVILLE

HOURS OF OPERATION
Sundays, 12 P.M. to 4 P.M.,
Memorial Day through
Labor Day

DIRECTIONS
From Tacoma, take SR 16
to SR 3. Take the exit for
Bainbridge Island and follow
signs for SR 305 north. Turn
left on SR 307 at the sign for
Hansville. Turn right on Point
No Point Road and park in
the dirt lot at the end of the
road. It's a short walk to
the lighthouse.

The lighthouse began service in 1880 at the point where Admiralty Inlet pours into Puget Sound. A fifth-order lens was mounted in a short brick tower, and a fogbell sounded warnings when visibility was poor. Quarters for two keepers were located south of the lighthouse. In 1900 a foghouse was attached to the tower to hold machinery for the operation of a kerosene-fueled fog trumpet. A few years later the lens was upgraded to a fourth-order. The station was automated in the 1980s.

In 1997 the lighthouse was leased to Kitsap County Parks, which offers tours of the lighthouse and also rents the keepers' quarters as a private residence.

Point No Point Light's first keeper hung a house lantern in the tower for several weeks until the fifth-order lens arrived in February 1880. The current fourth-order lens, installed in 1915, continues to operate. A bolt of lightning is thought to have shaken the lantern and cracked one bull's eye. *Elinor De Wire*

Point Robinson Light Station
VASHON

FOR MORE INFORMATION
Keepers of Point Robinson
P.O. Box 13234
Burton, WA 98013
www.ptrobinson.org
For rental information, call
206.463.9602

HOURS OF OPERATION
Volunteers with the Keepers
of Point Robinson offer tours
of the lighthouse on Sundays,
12 P.M. to 4 P.M., Memorial Day
through Labor Day.

DIRECTIONS
From Point Defiance in
Tacoma, take the ferry to
Vashon Island. Turn left onto
Vashon Highway and follow
the highway to a right turn
on Quartermaster Road. Turn
right onto Dockton Road. At
the Y, bear left onto Point
Robinson Road and continue
to the lighthouse.

Established in 1885 as a fog signal station, the Point Robinson steam whistle helped ships navigate the East Passage between Seattle and Tacoma. A single dwelling for the fog signal keeper was built south of the fog signal. In 1891 a 25-foot post mounted with a lens-lantern was added, but proved too short to be seen over the trees. Three years later it was relocated to a taller, wooden scaffold tower. The additional work created by the light required a second keeper, whose dwelling was built in 1907. The light and fog signal were combined into one structure in 1915.

The station was automated in the 1980s and later leased to Vashon Park District, which operates a vacation rental in one of the keepers' dwellings.

In 1894, Point Robinson had a scaffold tower and a small lens-lantern. By 1914, a light tower and attached foghouse were added. A coal cart sits next to the tower. The small red-roofed building is the oilhouse.
Jonathan De Wire

Coast Guard Archives

SPEND THE NIGHT AT A LIGHT

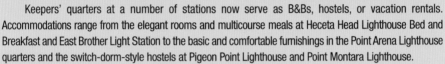

As lighthouses were automated and de-staffed by the Coast Guard in the 1980s, new uses were found for them. A popular conversion made the lighthouse an overnight experience. The lure of spending a night under the light and walking in the footsteps of yesterday's lightkeepers proved a profitable attraction.

Keepers' quarters at a number of stations now serve as B&Bs, hostels, or vacation rentals. Accommodations range from the elegant rooms and multicourse meals at Heceta Head Lighthouse Bed and Breakfast and East Brother Light Station to the basic and comfortable furnishings in the Point Arena Lighthouse quarters and the switch-dorm-style hostels at Pigeon Point Lighthouse and Point Montara Lighthouse.

One of the more unique experiences is offered at New Dungeness Light Station on the Strait of Juan de Fuca, Washington. The 1857 lighthouse sits in a wildlife refuge at the end of a long sand spit facing British Columbia. It is accessed only by foot or, at low tide, in the station's special four-wheel vehicles. No other vehicular travel is permitted.

"Keepers," as the volunteer staff call themselves, have one-week assignments at the site. They live in the modernized dwelling and do regular maintenance, upkeep, and public tours. Visitors arrive on foot, trekking 11 miles roundtrip to see the lighthouse. They can climb the tower, tour the small interpretive center, and have a picnic on the lawn. There is a restroom and fresh water on the grounds.

Though the beacon at New Dungeness Light Station operates automatically, volunteer crews have plenty of work to do to keep the station shipshape. At the same time, they can relax with books, puzzles, and other restful activities, and enjoy the pristine surroundings of snow-capped mountains, wheeling seabirds, and a rookery of seals. One entry in the station logbook calls the experience "peacefully rejuvenating."

New Dungeness Light Station was one of the first in the nation to transfer its daily duties from U.S. Coast Guard keepers to volunteer civilian keepers. It began this tradition in 1994 and considers the effort a special form of "living history." The Coast Guard maintains the beacon; volunteers take care of everything else. Perhaps the best part of the endeavor is the camaraderie and shared commitment of saving an important piece of history.

Like lightkeepers of old, volunteer keeper Mel Jetter takes down the flag at dusk at New Dungeness Light Station in Washington. The station, though automated, is staffed year-round. *Elinor De Wire*

Point Wilson Light Station
PORT TOWNSEND

The lighthouse opened in 1879 to guide ships through an important turn on the route from the Strait of Juan de Fuca to Puget Sound. It also served as a beacon for the busy harbor at Port Townsend. A fourth-order Fresnel lens was exhibited from a square tower jutting from the roof of the keeper's dwelling. The station also included a fog whistle. Ruby panels were installed on the lens in 1894 to differentiate the beacon from nearby lights.

A new 46-foot lighthouse with a foghouse was built in 1914. A keeper manned the station until it was automated in 1976. The lighthouse is part of Fort Worden State Park.

HOURS OF OPERATION
The lighthouse is open for tours Sundays, mid May through Labor Day, courtesy of a local Coast Guard flotilla. The surrounding park grounds are open year-round during daylight hours.

DIRECTIONS
From Main Street in Port Townsend, follow signs for Fort Worden State Park and the lighthouse.

Summer evening sunlight washes Point Wilson Light Station at Fort Worden. The 1914 lighthouse is the tallest in Puget Sound. The house dates back to 1979 when the station first opened. *Elinor De Wire*

FLOATING LIGHTHOUSES

In some shipping lanes, dangers existed far offshore and could not be marked by lighthouses. The lightship was developed to respond to this need. A combination of ship and lighthouse, it was anchored at perilous points in the sea-lanes where shallows, rocks, and shoals surreptitiously languished just beneath the surface. With a go-nowhere mission and a small crew to tend the light and fog signal, its warning to other vessels was a simple "steer clear of me."

The first patented lightship design was the *Nore*, anchored in England's Thames River estuary in 1731. It was a small wooden boat with an oil lamp hung from a single mast. Less than a century later,

The Columbia River's old wooden lightship took an amazing overland journey in 1899 after it ran aground and had to be refloated. *Coast Guard Archives*

the first lightships appeared in the United States at Willoughby Spit, Virginia, and Northeast Pass, Louisiana. They too were small boats with single lighted masts. A lamplighter rowed out to each vessel nightly to kindle the beacon and returned at dawn to extinguish it.

In the 1840s, revenue cutters were refitted as lightships and permanent crews were enlisted. By the 1860s, two sizes of lightships were in use. Small vessels weighed 100 tons or less; larger lightships were as heavy as 300 tons. "Inside" lightships served in rivers, bays, and sounds. "Outside" lightships were anchored off coastlines, sometimes miles at sea.

Lightships wore the names of the stations where they anchored and had a numbering system so they could easily be identified. On the West Coast they served at five outside locations—Umatilla Reef, Swiftsure Bank, and the Columbia River in Washington, and Blunts Reef and San Francisco in California. Relief lightships were towed from station to station to do substitute duty when the regular vessels were sent into port for maintenance or repair.

Lightships were designed to remain in one spot. Bulky, flattened hulls with bilge keels reduced rolling in heavy seas, and huge mushroom-shaped anchors held the vessels in position, digging firmly into the seabed. Heavy storms sometimes dragged the anchor or parted its chain, setting a lightship adrift.

The Columbia River Lightship No. 50 was torn from its station during a storm in November 1899. It broke anchor, drifted, and went aground on Cape Disappointment. The government gave it up for lost, but a house-moving company in Portland, Oregon, hoisted it onto a railway car and moved it a mile overland to Bakers Bay, where it was refloated and placed back in service.

Lightship duty was tedious and sometimes dangerous. Crews of 6 to 12 men, nicknamed "fish," lived on board in crowded quarters and worked long hours without any change in scenery. Storms could be terrifying. Fogbells and horns deprived crewmembers of sleep. Seasickness affected many, since lightships rolled constantly. Like all seamen, the crews missed their families during the long weeks of duty at sea.

The signature of the lightship was its light basket, which the men tended daily. Most vessels had two masts and two baskets, mounted near the top of each mast. Gimbaled oil lamps in the baskets remained level as the ship rolled. These were filled on deck, then hoisted up the masts on their own little pulley systems. Later, gas and electric lights with small lenses increased brilliance.

The dangers of lightship duty and the expense of operating lightships encouraged the development of other technologies to mark offshore perils. By 1987 all lightships in the United States were retired. Those on the West Coast were replaced by large navigation buoys. Three defunct lightships now sit in museums.

The Overfalls lightship that once served off Delaware is now owned by the U.S. Lighthouse Society and is berthed in Oakland, California. The Columbia River Maritime Museum at Astoria, Oregon, displays one of the river's lightships, and Northwest Seaport in Seattle owns one of the Swiftsure vessels.

Turn Point Light Station
ROCHE HARBOR

DIRECTIONS
The lighthouse is closed at present, but the grounds are open as part of a state preserve. It can be accessed by boat. Charters are available in Deer Harbor on Orcas Island and Friday Harbor on San Juan Island. Boats can drop anchor at Prevost Harbor and visitors then walk a 2-mile trail to the lighthouse.

Named for the point where ships make an important turn between Boundary Pass and Haro Strait, the light began operation in 1893 as a lens-lantern mounted on a foghouse for a steam whistle. A spacious dwelling for two keepers sat on the hill behind the light. In the 1930s the beacon was upgraded and moved to a small concrete tower in front of the fog signal building, which was also improved with a new electric horn. The station was automated in 1974 and solarized a few years later. The property has been transferred to the Bureau of Land Management, which plans to restore the buildings and open the site to the public.

Small but important, the beacon at Turn Point on Stuart Island was often upstaged by the fog signal. Keepers spent most of their time working in the foghouse but climbed the small ladder on the tower each day to check the light. **Above:** *Coast Guard Archives* **Left:** *Coast Guard Museum NW*

West Point Light Station
SEATTLE

The lighthouse was placed in operation in 1881 at the base of Magnolia Hill to guide ships into Elliott Bay. The 27-foot tower exhibited a fourth-order Fresnel lens. Behind it, a fogbell that had formerly served at Cape Disappointment hung in a wooden scaffold. In 1887, when the bell was replaced by a coal-fired steam fog trumpet, a foghouse was added to the tower.

A fort grew up on the bluff behind the lighthouse by 1900, and in 1915 the Lake Washington Ship Canal opened, increasing the light's importance. The station was automated in 1985—the last one in Washington to be de-staffed—and given a new electric foghorn. In 2004 the site was transferred to Seattle Parks and Recreation, which plans to open it for public use.

DIRECTIONS
The site is not open to the public at present but can be viewed from the beach in Discovery Park. Visitors can walk or bike to the beach from the parking area. In summer a shuttle bus runs from the parking area to the beach.

By 1930, when this photo of West Point Light was taken, there was ample evidence of dwindling salmon numbers in Puget Sound. A marker near the lighthouse door delineates the boundary of a salmon preserve.
U.S. Lighthouse Society

Chapter 4

Lighthouses of Alaska

The first known lighthouse on the Pacific Coast was a crude beacon placed in the cupola of the Russian governor's house at Sitka in 1837. When the United States purchased Alaska 30 years later, the small light was transferred to the U.S. Lighthouse Board and a keeper was paid 40 cents a day to maintain it. The beacon lasted only a decade more before the governor's house burned down.

The U.S. Navy then transferred the beacon to nearby Vitskari Island to better serve mariners. In 1894 the Sitka beacon was relighted on a post at the site where the original light had stood. It was a memorial of sorts, but also an aid to vessels entering the harbor. Until the twentieth century, these two beacons were the only lights guiding the way to America's "Ice Box."

Despite good intentions, the Lighthouse Board paid little attention to the nation's biggest territory until gold was discovered. Beginning in 1897, thousands of fortune-seekers headed to Alaska via the only route possible at the time—the watery highway from Seattle through the notoriously dangerous Inside Passage to Juneau. Blinded by frequent storms and fog, ships negotiated a patchwork of islands and rocks with only buoys to guide them. At the same time, Alaskan fishermen began lobbying for lights off of Kodiak Island and the Aleutians, citing the potential profits to be made in salmon and halibut fishing.

The cry for lighthouses reached fever pitch in 1901 when the steamship *Islander* went down off Douglas Island with $2 million in gold in her hold. More wrecks followed when reports of huge gold strikes sent thousands of people north in anything that would float. Despite a shortage of funds, the U.S. Lighthouse Board was forced to act. Ten lighthouses were built between 1902 and 1910.

Most of those early–twentieth century lighthouses were designed by Carl Leick, the board's primary architect for the Pacific Northwest region. Although Leick had achieved success building lighthouses in Oregon and Washington, the rush to mark Alaska's shores tested his mettle. Lack of funding and problems getting materials and crews to isolated sites resulted in poor construction that doomed many of the towers.

Lightkeepers faced even tougher challenges. The board had difficulty recruiting men to serve at the lonely outposts. Although families lived at lighthouses situated near towns, most of the sites were "stag stations," the board's description for those so remote and dangerous that only men could live there. Special incentives, such as higher pay and more leave, attracted men to these far-flung assignments.

Flaming twilight bathes Five Finger Light Station in the summer of 1984, shortly before the lighthouse was unmanned. *U.S. Coast Guard*

By 1920 many of Alaska's hastily constructed sentinels were crumbling. One by one, all but Eldred Rock Lighthouse were rebuilt. Reinforced concrete proved the best material—cheap, durable, and strong. The popular style of the period was an art deco or moderne design with clean lines and simple ornaments. Optics and fog signal equipment were upgraded, and living conditions for the keepers were improved.

By the time the U.S. Coast Guard assumed control of the lighthouses in 1939, many had radiobeacons. During World War II, LORAN (Long Range Navigation) was added. These invisible forms of silent signaling vastly improved marine safety in Alaska and allowed ships to find their positions in even the worst weather and sea conditions.

After World War II, a move to economize and streamline the lighthouse service was in full swing. Alaska's lighthouses were among the first in the nation to be automated and unmanned. Priority was given to the most isolated and difficult-to-access sites. The sentinels at Scotch Cap and Cape Sarichef, near the tip of the Aleutian Islands, were the most remote and vulnerable to natural catastrophes, such as ice fogs and tsunamis. By the 1970s, self-sufficient skeleton-tower beacons that required maintenance only once each year marked these sites.

As Alaska's lighthouses were being unmanned and closed, local residents rallied to save them from decay. The Alaska Lighthouse Association, based in Douglas, dedicated its energies to the preservation of Point Retreat Lighthouse. Both the Alaska Lighthouse Association and the Juneau Lighthouse Association provide information about lighthouses in the state. To learn more about boat and seaplane trips to the lighthouses, visit their website www.aklighthouse.org or write Alaska Lighthouse Association, P.O. Box 240149, Douglas, AK 99824. Contact the Juneau Lighthouse Association at P.O. Box 022262, Juneau, AK 99802.

The Russian Governor's house in Sitka, known as Baranov's Castle, held the first light on the West Coast. Though crude, it served fur trading vessels entering the foggy and sometimes stormy port. *Alaska State Library*

Cape Decision Light Station
SITKA

The last light station established in Alaska was at Cape Decision, about 85 miles southeast of Sitka. It sits on Kiui Island, where Chatham and Sumner straits meet. The lighthouse went into service in 1932 with a third-order Fresnel lens, primarily to assist fishing vessels.

The 40-foot reinforced-concrete tower, rising from a dwelling, was manned until 1974. The classical lens was moved to Clausen Museum in Petersburg and a modern beacon was installed. The lighthouse remains in service today, but is not open to the public.

As fish canneries grew along the waterways near Sitka, it became clear that a lighthouse was needed. Cape Decision Light went into service in 1932 with quarters for three keepers. Like many other Alaskan lights, it was a stag station that allowed only men. *Coast Guard Archives*

Cape Hinchenbrook Lighthouse
CORDOVA

The first lighthouse to mark the cape was a two-story octagonal dwelling with a tower rising from the roof. It stood on an island at the entrance to Prince William Sound and warned of the dangerous Seal Rocks. Though it went into service in 1910, within a decade earthquakes tore away the cliff on which the lighthouse perched and forced construction of a new lighthouse farther inland.

The second tower was completed in 1934 and is a reinforced-concrete dwelling with a 67-foot tower attached to one side. It was automated in 1974. The lighthouse continues in service but is not open to the public.

The wilderness of Alaska is evident in this 1950s photo of Cape Hinchenbrook Light Station. Its keepers coped with wolves and bears. Most Alaskan lightkeepers were issued rifles, which they hung over entrance doors for quick access. *U.S. Coast Guard*

Cape Spencer Light Station
JUNEAU

The lighthouse sits on an island at the entrance to Cross Sound, west of Juneau. Built in 1925, its purpose was to aid vessels through Icy Strait, a safer route than the tumultuous Outside Passage. It is a reinforced-concrete dwelling with a 25-foot tower rising from the roof. The original optic was a third-order Fresnel lens, given to the Alaska State Museum in 1974, when the station was automated. A modern beacon now shines from the tower. The light station is not open to the public.

Cape Spencer was one of the most isolated assignments in the nation. Keepers had a 20-mile trip by boat to get mail. The closest town was 150 miles away. Just getting into the boat was a challenge, and a crane was used to lower keepers into it. *Coast Guard Archives*

The Tsunami at Scotch Cap

At the western end of the Aleutian Islands, off the Alaskan coast, lies a dismal outpost called Unimak Island—known among lightkeepers as the "Roof of Hell." It's a land of rumbling volcanoes, ice fogs, and frigid winds. This gateway between the North Pacific Ocean and the Bering Sea saw hundreds of shipwrecks during the mad gold rush to Nome. On a windswept point called Scotch Cap, a lighthouse was built in 1903 to help avert those disasters. It was the outermost sentinel in the nation at the time, and a dreaded assignment.

At first only two keepers stood watch on the distant sentinel, but when the Coast Guard took over the station in 1939, they assigned five men to the square tower and built a Direction Finding Station (DFS) high on the ridge behind the lighthouse. It was lonely work. The nearest village was more than 100 miles away and the supply ship came infrequently, often delayed by bad weather.

On April 1, 1946, disaster struck the lighthouse. In the early hours of darkness an earthquake rumbled beneath the island, a slight shudder that lasted only a few seconds. A weak aftershock came a short time later. The man on watch at Scotch Cap Lighthouse dutifully recorded the events in the station logbook and radioed the watchman at the DFS on the hill. He too had felt the tremors. Both men thought little more about the event, since the epicenter of the quake seemed far away and no damage had occurred.

Hours passed, and then the watchman at the DFS heard a strange rustling sound outside, like a great waterfall cascading in the distance. The hissing grew louder and closer, and then it became a roar. Moments later a massive wave struck the lighthouse, swept up the hill, and sent seawater swirling over the floor in the DFS. It was a tsunami—a giant wave spawned by an undersea earthquake—and it caused a huge rock shelf in the Aleutian Trench to break off in a massive submarine landslide.

The sturdy, concrete lighthouse at Scotch Cap in the Aleutians was no match for a 1946 tsunami. The station was destroyed and its keepers were killed. *Coast Guard Archives*

A column of sea water above the quake was charged with energy that could only dissipate in the form of a wave. Hardly perceptible in the open ocean, the wave advanced toward the island at a speed of 500 miles per hour. As it reached the shallows off Scotch Cap it slowed and telescoped in size. By the time it came crashing down on the lighthouse it had grown to a monstrous 100 feet tall.

The wave knocked out electricity at the DFS and extinguished the beam from the lighthouse. The crew rounded up flashlights to check for damage. They repeatedly radioed the lighthouse, but there was no answer, nor were there any lights or signs of activity in the darkness below. Fearing the worst, they radioed the Coast Guard station at Ketchikan: "Light extinguished and horn silent."

As dawn slowly crept over the island, the fate of the five keepers at Scotch Cap Light became apparent. All that remained of the lighthouse was a jumble of twisted wreckage. The foundation had been wiped almost clean. The DFS crew thoroughly searched the station and the surrounding shore, but found no bodies. Human remains washed up on the beach a few days later.

A new lighthouse was built in 1950, much higher on the point, where seismic waves cannot reach it. On the wall of the lighthouse a memorial plaque commemorates the sacrifices of the five Scotch Cap lightkeepers. To avert future tragedy, a warning system was installed at key points along the Pacific Rim, including Palmer, Alaska. Its job is to alert tsunami-prone areas when a seismic event occurs and large waves are imminent. Had it been in service on April 1, 1946, perhaps the lighthouse crew could have escaped death.

Cape St. Elias Lighthouse
CORDOVA

FOR MORE INFORMATION
Cape St. Elias Lightkeepers
Association
P.O. Box 1023
Cordova, AK 99574
907.424.5182
e-mail
jbocci@alaskalighthouse.org

Guarding the south end of Kayak Island, 65 miles from Cordova, the Cape St. Elias lighthouse was opened in 1916. The 55-foot tower, exhibiting a third-order lens, was attached to a foghouse. It overlooks forbidding Pinnacle Rock. Behind the station rises St. Elias Mountain.

The dwelling and boathouse remain intact, but the buildings have stood empty since automation in 1974. A modern solar optic has replaced the classical lens. The lens is on display at the Cordova Museum. The station is accessible and open to the public via seaplane.

The keepers of the bleak and far-flung Cape St. Elias Light Station were men of mettle, whose sanity was tested daily. Not all of them coped; in 1949 one wild-eyed keeper rowed out to sea and never returned. *Coast Guard Archives*

Rusted and weatherworn after automation in 1974, Cape St. Elias Light kept its lens for a time before the classical optic was removed and replaced with a modern beacon. *Toni Bocci*

Eldred Rock Light Station
JUNEAU

Some 50 miles north of Juneau is Eldred Rock Light Station, a beacon for the Lynn Canal. The octagonal two-story dwelling with a tower rising from the roof was built in 1906 and is the oldest original lighthouse still standing in Alaska. The lower level is reinforced concrete, while the second story and tower are wood. The station's original fourth-order lens was replaced by a smaller modern optic in 1973. The lens is now in the Sheldon Museum at Haines. The light station is not open to the public.

Several shipwrecks spurred the construction of Eldred Rock Lighthouse in Lynn Canal, pictured here around 1920. The worst was the February 1898 loss of the *Clara Nevada*, which caught fire during a storm, burned, and sank in the shallows off the rock. *Coast Guard Archives*

Five Finger Islands Light Station
JUNEAU

FOR MORE INFORMATION
The Juneau Lighthouse
Association
10945 Glacier Highway
Juneau, AK 99801
e-mail
juneaulight@earthlink.net
www.5fingerlighthouse.com

Located on a small island in the north end of Frederick Sound, the lighthouse was established in 1902 and was lighted the same day as Sentinel Island Lighthouse. The two lighthouses were the first sentinels in Alaska. The lighthouse at Five Finger Islands showed a fourth-order lens from a small tower atop the two-story dwelling.

The station burned in 1933. A second tower of reinforced concrete replaced it three years later. The 68-foot tower was automated in 1984—the last Alaskan lighthouse to be de-staffed. It remains in operation but is not open to the public.

The original Five Finger Islands Light Station burned to the ground in December 1933 when keepers tried to thaw frozen pipes using a blow torch. *Coast Guard Archives*

Five Finger Islands Light's concrete tower, built in 1936, was considerably more comfortable than the rustic 1902 sentinel it replaced. *U.S. Coast Guard*

Guards Island Lighthouse

KETCHIKAN

Established in 1904, the lighthouse stands on an island 12 miles northwest of Ketchikan, where Clarence Strait meets Tongass Narrows. Originally, a square wooden tower with a fogbell and a fourth-order beacon served here. It was one of only a few Alaskan lighthouses to accommodate wives and children.

In 1924 the structure was razed and replaced by a reinforced-concrete light tower and foghouse. The station was automated in 1969. Still active today, it operates a modern beacon. The lighthouse is not open to the public.

The small Coast Guard community on Guard Islands Light in 1951 occupied one of the loneliest spots on the West Coast. In 1966, a local hunter gave the all-male crew a fawn, which they tamed and raised. "Wickie" had free run of the station and slept at the foot of one man's bed. *U.S. Coast Guard*

Mary Island Lighthouse
KETCHIKAN

Built in 1903 a few miles south of Ketchikan, this station consisted of an octagonal dwelling surmounted by a tower. The lantern held a fourth-order lens. The wooden tower deteriorated quickly and a new lighthouse was planned.

Built in 1938, it was the last lighthouse constructed in Alaska. The reinforced-concrete tower was attached to a foghouse. The station was automated in 1969 with a modern beacon, and the classical lens was given to the Douglas-Juneau Museum in Juneau. The lighthouse is not open to the public.

Three lighthouses mark the island-riddled seaway to the busy port of Ketchikan. Mary Island's 1938 tower was the last lighthouse built in Alaska. *Coast Guard Archives*

Point Retreat Lighthouse
JUNEAU

In 1904 a lens-lantern beacon on a short tower was built on the northern point of Mansfield Peninsula on Admiralty Island. Two keepers' dwellings completed the small light station. Within a few years the light was downgraded and automated. By 1920, increased shipping spurred construction of a new, more powerful lighthouse.

A 25-foot reinforced-concrete tower and square foghouse were built in 1924. A radiobeacon was added a few years later. In the late 1950s the lens and lantern were removed and replaced by a minor beacon. The station was automated and unmanned in 1973.

The lighthouse is not open to the public but the Alaska Lighthouse Association is restoring it and hopes to open it for tours in 2006.

Several minor lights were established in Alaska in 1904, including one at Point Retreat. In 1923 it was modernized with the addition of a block tower (right). A 1961 photo (above) shows the station during its last years before automation. *Coast Guard Archives*

Sentinel Island Lighthouse
JUNEAU

FOR MORE INFORMATION
Gastineau Channel
Historical Society
P.O. Box 021264
Juneau, AK 99802
For tour information, call
907.586.5338

DIRECTIONS
The lighthouse is visible from
shore 29 miles north of Juneau
on Highway 7.

A marker for Frederick Sound and Lynn Canal, the lighthouse went into service in 1902, on the same day as Five Finger Islands Lighthouse. The handsome sentinel consisted of a two-story wooden house with a tower attached to the front. It showed a fourth-order Fresnel lens.

A modern, reinforced-concrete sentinel replaced it in 1935. The lantern from the original tower was placed on the new lighthouse. The station was automated in 1966 and is still an active aid to navigation.

The lighthouse was given to the Gastineau Channel Historical Society in 2004. Currently they are rehabilitating the station for public use. The lighthouse is accessible by tour boat but the tower is not yet open.

Working in tandem with Five Finger Islands Light, the beacon at Sentinel Island provides safe passage between Wrangell and Skagway. *Courtesy of Robert Sears*

Tree Point Lighthouse
KETCHIKAN

L ocated only 7 miles north of the Canadian border, the first lighthouse at this site was an octagonal foghouse with a tower rising from its roof. It began operation in 1903 with a third-order Fresnel lens to guide shipping between Prince Rupert and Ketchikan.

In 1935 a new, 58-foot, reinforced-concrete lighthouse replaced the original structure. It was automated in 1969 but was discontinued a few years later. It is the only existing lighthouse in Alaska that is no longer active. The site is located in a remote area of Misty Fjords National Monument. The tower is not open to the public.

Despite its modern appearance, Tree Point Lighthouse had no on-site water supply during the years keepers lived on station. A pipeline brought water from a lake two miles away to fill a concrete cistern.
Coast Guard Archives

Chapter 5

Lighthouses of Hawaiʻi

The Sandwich Islands, as Hawaiʻi was once called, were the maritime crossroads of the Pacific in the nineteenth century. Ships used the islands as an idyllic stopover for rest, repair, and provisions. Islanders knew their coastline well and rarely ventured far from shore. Simple bonfires served their needs and those of occasional visiting ships. But when the lucrative whaling industry arose in the 1820s, the need for lighthouses became paramount.

The Hawaiians lacked the materials and skill to build lighthouses, but by 1840 King Kamehameha III had gathered the resources necessary to erect a wooden light tower at Lahaina, Maui. Twenty-nine years later, Honolulu merchants and ship owners built a tiny wooden lighthouse on pilings in the harbor channel. Nicknamed "The Harbor Wink" for its petite size, it stood 26 feet tall and had a fourth-order Fresnel lens.

Though many of Hawaiʻi's early lights were crude structures, no expense was spared in construction of Makapuʻu Point Light in 1909. Its 12-foot, hyper radiant lens, with 1,140 prisms, is the largest in the nation. *Jonathan De Wire*

By 1900, light towers also stood at Barbers Point and Diamond Head on Oʻahu, and at Nāwiliwili, Kauaʻi. Most were mutually maintained by shipping interests and the Hawaiian government.

Though Hawaiʻi became a territory of the United States in 1898, improvement of navigational aids did not begin in the islands until 1904. Even then, progress was slow. All of the existing lights needed repairs or rebuilding, and a number of sites were identified for new lights. The lightkeepers were untrained, unsupervised, poorly paid local citizens appointed by the Hawaiian government.

Despite overwhelming agreement in Congress that Hawaiʻi needed better navigational aids, little money was allocated for this purpose. Perhaps the remoteness of this new territory made it difficult for Americans to fully embrace it. A lighthouse district was created for the islands, but the meager resources set aside for construction resulted in a string of unsophisticated, poorly constructed lights.

With the burgeoning sugar cane industry on Kauaʻi in the 1890s, a good light was needed at Nāwiliwili Harbor. Two wooden lights preceded the current concrete tower on Ninini Point. *U.S. Coast Guard*

Most lighthouses were simple wooden-trestle towers with a small lens-lantern, accessed by ladder. Local men continued to serve as keepers. Some walked many miles to tend the beacons, which were usually situated on lonely capes and headlands where no one lived. Deliveries of oil, supplies, and paychecks were sporadic at best. The remarkable resourcefulness and solicitude of the islanders is what kept the lights burning.

With the opening of the Panama Canal in 1914, Hawai'i was catapulted into the modern maritime era. World War I underscored the importance of the islands in a global conflict. These events, and complaints about Hawai'i's crude lighthouses, finally convinced Congress to authorize large sums of money for new construction.

Reinforced concrete and steel in slightly modified pyramidal concrete designs became the mainstays of lighthouse construction in Hawai'i after the war. Skeleton towers, with less resistance to wind and waves than masonry towers, were ideal for Hawai'i's storm-prone shores. A supply tender named *Kukui*, meaning "light," was assigned to the lighthouse district in Honolulu and regularly visited the sentinels to provide provisions and maintain them.

Equally important was the attention the Bureau of Lighthouses gave to lightkeepers and their families. They built on-site dwellings with reliable water systems. Lightkeepers received better training and a pay increase. Towers were outfitted with the most modern optics and direction-finding equipment. To solve the problem of staffing isolated sites, remote spots—such as the islet of Lehua and Ka'ula Rock in the western end of the island chain near Ni'ihau—featured self-sufficient acetylene gas lights.

A corps of lights and keepers emerged to rival any in the continental United States. Within a few years, Coast Guard automation efforts further modernized and streamlined existing Hawaiian lighthouses while adding new beacons to far-flung places in the archipelago.

Today only a few traditional light towers remain in the islands. Visitors often pass by the smaller concrete and skeleton towers without recognizing them as lighthouses. The oversight is due, in part, to the Aloha State's belated interest in its lighthouses—structures that only recently have drawn interest from historians and the state department of tourism. To date, no statewide group has formed to preserve lighthouses. The Hawai'i Maritime Center, located in the Aloha Tower (a navigational beacon itself) is working toward that goal.

Desperate for a light to mark busy Honolulu Harbor, shipping interests funded the tiny "Harbor Wink" light in 1869 to replace a crude oil lamp wrapped with red cloth. A local newspaper derisively called it "an infantile structure" and "a bird cage."
Coast Guard Archives

THE LIGHTHOUSE PELE SPARED

Pele, the Polynesian goddess of fire, is legendary in Hawaii. Moody and miserable, she is said to dwell in the fire pit of Kilauea, the Big Island's most active volcano. On most days, Pele quietly sleeps deep below the earth, but occasionally she wakes and tosses her lava-red hair over the landscape.

Early on the morning of January 30, 1960, Pele stirred from her slumber in Kilauea's East Rift. Molten rock spurted upward in a curtain of fire, and a wall of hot, slow-moving lava made its way down the mountain, devastating the surrounding landscape. In its path was the 124-foot skeleton lighthouse at Cape Kumukahi.

The Coast Guard evacuated the entire crew at the station except for the officer in charge, Joseph Estrella. Within days, Estella was also forced to leave. By February 2, lava had buried the two keepers' homes and was moving toward the tower. Local islanders carried offerings of food and liquor to the volcano to mollify Pele and remind her of the benevolent mission of the lighthouse.

As Pele's fiery lava inched closer to the lighthouse, everyone feared the worst. The electrical wiring in the tower melted and its beacon, which Estrella had switched to automatic operation, went out. But when the wall of molten rock was within ten feet of the lighthouse, it split and forked around the tower.

When Pele's fury abated, people began speculating about this curious turn of fate. The Coast Guard crew quickly dubbed Cape Kumukahi the "Lucky Lighthouse." It was repaired and automated. The destroyed homes were not rebuilt.

Local residents weren't so sure luck had saved the lighthouse, however. To this day, many people still contend Pele heard the prayers and spared the lighthouse because of its good work.

Barbers Point Lighthouse
Makakilo, O'ahu

DIRECTIONS
The lighthouse is located at the end of Olai Street, off Highway 95 near the Barbers Point Naval Air Station. The site is open, but the tower is closed.

The first lighthouse at this site was a 40-foot stone tower built in 1888. It showed a fourth-order Fresnel lens and warned vessels away from a dangerous reef about 10 miles west of the entrance to Pearl Harbor. At the time, it was the tallest lighthouse in Hawai'i. As the shoreline developed, however, the light became harder to see.

A 71-foot, reinforced-concrete tower was built to replace it in 1933. The lens was moved to the new tower and electrified. In 1964 the lantern was removed and the light was automated with an aerobeacon. A high-intensity double-barrel beacon was installed in 1985. It still serves marine traffic.

Kalaeloa Reef was the scene of numerous shipwrecks before construction of Barbers Point Light in 1888. The lantern was removed in 1964 to make way for a modern beacon. *Courtesy of Kim Halstead*

By the 1930s, a new concrete tower had been built at Barbers Point. It was painted in a camouflage pattern during World War II. *Coast Guard Archives*

Cape Kumukahi Lighthouse
PAHOA, HAWAI'I

DIRECTIONS
The lighthouse is not open for tours but can be viewed at the end of Route 132 (an unpaved road), about 15 miles east of Pahoa.

An automatic acetylene gas light on a 32-foot wooden tower was the first beacon on this windy, Big Island cape. It served only five years before it was replaced by a 125-foot steel skeleton tower topped with a powerful aerobeacon. The keepers lived in two comfortable dwellings about a half-mile from the lighthouse.

Eruptions from nearby Kilauea Volcano endangered the lighthouse on several occasions. The most serious threat occurred in January 1960, when an advancing lava flow burned down the dwellings and caused the fuel tanks to explode. The skeleton tower was not damaged and was returned to service a few weeks later as an automatic beacon. Today it is the most powerful lighthouse in Hawai'i.

The steel light tower at Cape Kumukahi lacks beauty but has an engaging history. It escaped harm in a 1964 volcanic eruption. Black rubble from the lava flow was still visible in this photo from 1984. *Elinor De Wire*

Diamond Head Lighthouse
HONOLULU, O'AHU

In 1899 a 40-foot lighthouse was built on the southern slope of Hawai'i's most famous landmark—Diamond Head. The truncated square tower was a framework of iron enclosing stone walls. The lantern showed a third-order Fresnel lens. It was rebuilt in 1918 to a height of 57 feet, and a spacious keeper's dwelling was added. Six years later the light was automated, but the third-order lens remained in place. The quarters are now occupied by the commanding officer of the Fourteenth Coast Guard District.

DIRECTIONS
The lighthouse is on private property but can be viewed from a pullout a few hundred feet east of the tower on Diamond Head Road. It also can be seen from a lookout atop Diamond Head Crater.

Visitors to Hawai'i's extinct volcanic crater at Diamond Head often unknowingly pass by its lighthouse. The comely sentinel stands amid palms on the south slope of the crater and sends a steady beam over dense coral beds. *Elinor De Wire*

Visitors on the Wing

M any Pacific Coast lighthouses stand in bird sanctuaries and rookeries, on wildlife refuges, and along the great avian migration routes. This is a bittersweet circumstance, for while birds are an interesting and welcome part of the lighthouse environment, they can cause problems.

Lighthouses are favorite resting spots for birds. Birds land on the towers and foul the railings, windows, decks, and roofs. Lightkeepers spent a good portion of their day cleaning bird droppings from the lantern. Where water was collected from rooftops and piped into cisterns for use by the lighthouse keepers, constant cleaning was required.

"When storm clouds were sighted, the whole family hauled out the buckets and soap," recalled a keeper's grandson at New Dungeness Light Station in Washington. The bird mess was hastily scrubbed away from the catchment area to prepare for the clean rainwater that would fill the cistern.

Birds find ample spots for nesting at light stations, sometimes in the worst places. In the days of oil lamps, small bird nests had to be cleared regularly from the ventilator in the cupola at Point Conception Lighthouse in California. A plugged ventilator interfered with the proper burning of the lamps.

Farther up the coast at East Brother Island Light Station near San Francisco, nesting in the foghorns was a problem. The horns were tested every autumn after a long summer of no fog. Birds and their nests would be blown out of the horns by the immense concussion of sound. Sometimes gulls crawled into the foghorns and died, creating a horrendous smell. The only way to dislodge them was to fire up the boiler and let the horns roar.

Lured by the light in a tall tower, or confused by it, birds often slam into lighthouses at night. Lightkeepers' logbooks are rife with such events. James Gibbs, who served on Tillamook Rock Lighthouse in 1945, wrote: "Sometimes they flew directly into the powerful beam in the calmest weather, but more frequently it was the stress of storms that claimed the greatest number. It is generally believed that they are blinded but . . . for no apparent reason they will dive at the light as if drawn by a magnet, attacking like a dive-bomber and shattering themselves against the panes of glass."

Smaller birds usually caused little trouble for the lightkeepers, beyond the mess involved in cleaning up feathers and blood. Some keepers considered the birds a perk. During World War I, when food rationing took place, a flock of ducks slammed Yaquina Head Lighthouse. There was no damage to the tower, and for several days afterward, keeper Fred Booth and his family feasted on roast duck, duck pot pie, and duck soup.

Large birds, however, could cause considerable damage if they collided with the lantern. In 1880 a flock of geese flew into the windows at Piedras Blancas Light in California. They shattered the lantern panes and chipped some prisms on the first-order lens. The cost for repairs ran several hundred dollars.

Bird hunting was routine for many lightkeepers and provided food at isolated stations where delivery of provisions could be held up by storms and heavy seas. Wild bird eggs comprised a great part

Birds, confused by bright beams, often flew into lighthouses. Logbooks contain frequent mention of these events, often with serious consequences for the birds and the light. *Elinor De Wire Collection*

of the lighthouse diet. Farallon Island Lighthouse off San Francisco has a huge seabird rookery surrounding it. Lightkeepers sometimes complained about the noise and smell of the birds but were thankful for the eggs. One man even sold seabird eggs to San Francisco bakeries to earn a second income. His enterprise angered the city's egg hunters, who felt the keeper had an advantage over them, living so close to the rookery. "Egg Wars" erupted, and the government intervened to cool down tempers.

In spite of the trouble birds caused, bird watching was a popular pastime for most lightkeepers. They kept lists of the kinds of birds they sighted, drew pictures of them, and sometimes conducted bird counts or collected specimens for scientists. Laura Hecox, keeper of Santa Cruz Lighthouse from 1883 to 1917, was an amateur zoologist who started a small museum of marine life in her home. It included a variety of local birds. A lightkeeper at Washington's Slip Point Lighthouse did taxidermy in his free time. Years after the lighthouse was decommissioned, his stuffed birds were discovered in the attic of the abandoned keeper's dwelling.

There were lonesome days too, when birds were beloved companions for lightkeepers. The men at Tillamook Rock Lighthouse were charmed by the swallows living in nooks and crannies near the offshore station. Their soft chatter and the tending of their young brightened an otherwise gray existence for the keepers: "The young swallow had her first fly today," one man wrote in the log. The men kept watch as she matured, nested, and raised her own babies. With no women allowed on the lighthouse, this tiny female's activities were cherished reminders of their loved ones ashore.

Kalaupapa, Lighthouse
KALAUPAPA, MOLOKA'I

A red lens-lantern on a 34-foot pole served as the first beacon on Makanalua Peninsula while a permanent light was under construction. Finished in 1909, the reinforced-concrete lighthouse rose 132 feet high and exhibited a second-order clamshell lens—the tallest and brightest beacon in Hawai'i at the time. It was nicknamed "The Lepers' Light," due to its proximity to the leprosarium at Kalaupapa.

The station was electrified in 1935 and, because of its isolation, it was automated in 1966. In the late 1980s the lens was removed and given to the Lahaina Restoration Foundation for display on Maui. An aerobeacon replaced the lens. Today the site is part of the Kalaupapa National Historic Park.

FOR MORE INFORMATION
Moloka'i Mule Ride
P.O. Box 200
Moloka'i, HI 96757
800.567.7550
e-mail muleman@aloha.net
www.molokai.com/muleride

DIRECTIONS
This lighthouse is difficult to access, but can be reached by mule train and a hike.

Concern over a nearby leprosarium dictated regulations for the keepers of Kalaupapa Light, who were instructed not to leave the station or allow visitors. The huge clamshell lens was nicknamed "The Leper's Light."
Right: *U.S. Coast Guard*
Opposite: *Coast Guard Archives*

Kilauea Point Lighthouse
KILAUEA, KAUA'I

FOR MORE INFORMATION
Kilauea National Wildlife Refuge
P.O. Box 87
Kilauea, HI 96754
800.828.1413
www.cr.nps.gov/maritime/light/
kilauea.htm

HOURS OF OPERATION
The site is open weekdays
during daylight hours.

DIRECTIONS
The lighthouse is at the end of
Kilauea Road, off Highway 56,
about 2 miles north of the
town of Kilauea.

The lighthouse was built in 1913 on the north shore of Kaua'i to serve ships arriving from the west. Though only 52 feet tall, the reinforced-concrete tower sat on a high bluff overlooking Moku'ae'ae Island. Its second-order clamshell lens sent a beam more than 20 miles seaward and became the major landfall light for sea traffic from the Far East. Two keepers' dwellings were built near the tower.

The station was automated in 1975. A year later, to facilitate easier maintenance, the lens was decommissioned and the beacon was transferred to a 10-foot pole in front of the tower. Today it is part of the Kilauea National Wildlife Refuge.

Called "The Great Eye of Kaua'i," Kilauea Point Lighthouse was the last traditional sentinel built in the islands. The cyclopean lens weighs five tons and cast a beam more than 20 miles out to sea before it was decommissioned in 1975. A modern pole beacon has taken its place. **Above:** *Courtesy of Kim Halstead* **Opposite:** *Elinor De Wire*

THE LIGHTKEEPER

The stereotype of the lighthouse keeper conjures an image of a wizened old man with white whiskers and sea legs, hobbling up and down the tower stairs to tend the lamps and look out to sea from his high perch, in search of a ship in distress. It's the romantic image we cherish today, but it's hardly accurate.

On the Pacific Coast, as in all regions of the nation, both men and women did the work. Most started their careers as young adults and, if they liked the job, stayed on into old age. Except at the most isolated stations, families were welcome. Wives and children were able helpers and sometimes had official, paid appointments as assistant keepers. A few women earned the coveted principle keeper's job heading up a station.

On the West Coast, lightkeepers were usually chosen from local communities. Customs officials in ports along the coast administered simple exams to applicants to be sure they could read and write and handle the necessary duties of keeping the light and fog signal. The U.S. Lighthouse Board gave the final approval for the hiring of all keepers. Pay was based on experience and the difficulty and isolation of the station where a keeper was assigned.

Keepers normally entered the service as third assistants, then worked their way through the ranks to principle keeper—those in charge of the stations. Typical pay for a head keeper in 1860 was about $650 per year. The Lighthouse Board also paid for moving expenses, and provided the keeper with a house, sometimes a horse and wagon or a boat, and some basic food provisions, such as flour, sugar, salted meat, and dried beans. All tools and equipment were provided, as was training to assure the station was properly run. There were few amenities. One perk was a folding bookcase with about 80 books. Dozens of these libraries were circulated among the lighthouses to assuage boredom and edify the ranks.

Representatives of the various lighthouse districts conducted regular inspections. They arrived at lighthouses in supply ships called tenders, and they scoured the stations with critical eyes. The logbook had to be well kept, the light and fog signal in good order, and everything at the site clean and shipshape, including the keepers' homes. This white-glove practice began in the 1850s, following a scathing period of criticism of the lighthouse service for being inferior to its counterpart agencies in Europe. In the 1870s the U.S. Lighthouse Board created a quasi-military corps of keepers by instituting uniforms with visible rank, and awards for excellent service.

Some keepers served long tenures, moving from lighthouse to lighthouse throughout their careers. The jobs were politically controlled until 1896, when lightkeepers were added to the list of government employees covered by civil service laws. In 1918 the board authorized a pension and set the mandatory retirement age at 75. When the U.S. Lighthouse Establishment was abolished in 1939 and the U.S. Coast Guard assumed control of lighthouses, the occupation became even more military. Also at this time, women were phased out of the work, since it had become increasingly mechanized and technical in the twentieth century and the Coast Guard did not train women for this type of work until much later.

Solicitous and dedicated, most lightkeepers were respected members of the community. The stern-faced crew of Cape Flattery Lighthouse is pictured about 1915. *Coast Guard Museum NW*

Coast Guard keepers usually were boatswains or electricians brought on to tend the lights. They rotated from station to station more frequently than past lighthouse service employees. Some men had their families at the station with them, while a few men served at "stag stations"—the term for lighthouses where only men were allowed to live. Coast Guard keepers also were responsible for more technological work, such as operating a radiobeacon or LORAN (Long Range Navigation) system.

Ultimately, as lighthouses became increasingly costly to staff, the Coast Guard installed automatic devices and removed the keepers from their posts. The last West Coast lighthouse keeper went off the payroll in 1987. This ended 140 years of lightkeeping on the Pacific Coast and closed an important chapter in lighthouse history.

Kauhola Point Lighthouse
KOHALA, HAWAI'I

DIRECTIONS
The lighthouse is located at the end of a rugged dirt road off Highway 270, about 5 miles east-southeast of the northernmost point of the island. The road is often traversable only by four-wheel-drive vehicle.

The original beacon was a lens-lantern placed atop a wood-frame tower in 1904 to mark the north shore of the Big Island. In 1917 the light was changed to a fourth-order Fresnel lens and moved to a taller wooden tower. A fire in 1923 put out the light and damaged the tower.

A new, 86-foot, reinforced-concrete lighthouse replaced it. Two electric airway beacons were mounted on the top, exhibiting an unusual beam of light that alternated red and green flashes. Recently the lantern was replaced with a rotating beacon.

A simple trestle tower held the light at Kauhola Point until a primary seacoast lighthouse was built in 1933. The new tower was the first in Hawai'i to exhibit a flashing red and green airway beacon. *Coast Guard Archives*

Lahaina Harbor Lighthouse
LAHAINA, MAUI

A 9-foot wooden light tower was built on the waterfront of this old whaling town in 1840 to aid ships as they entered the harbor. Two oil lamps were piggybacked in a boxlike lantern. The sentinel at Lahaina Harbor was the first lighthouse in Hawai'i. The tower was repaired several times before being replaced in 1866, and it was rebuilt again to a height of 55 feet in 1905.

DIRECTIONS
The lighthouse stands on the waterfront in the historic district of Lahaina. It is not open to the public.

Plans to automate many of Hawai'i's lighthouses resulted in the construction of a fourth, more modern lighthouse in 1917. The reinforced-concrete tower served as a model for many of Hawai'i's twentieth century lighthouses. It was a pyramidal-shaped tower with no lantern and an exposed automatic beacon fueled by acetylene tanks. Electrified in 1937, today it shows a red beacon visible for 7 miles.

Lahaina Light blends with the nautical theme on the waterfront of Maui's oldest whaling town. It has operated self-sufficiently since its construction in 1917. *Courtesy of Kim Halstead*

Makapu'u Point Lighthouse
WAIMANALO, O'AHU

DIRECTIONS
Take Highway 72 east of Honolulu to a parking area at the base of the cliff. Hike up the service road about a half-mile to the lighthouse. Caution: the hike is strenuous and the site is windy.

Built in 1909 to guide shipping into Honolulu from the east, the lighthouse was one of the most elevated in Hawai'i. It sat on a rock outcropping 400 feet above the sea. A dirt road led to the keepers' homes on top of the point. The lighthouse was accessed by a narrow trail cut into the cliff. The 46-foot brick tower exhibited the nation's only hyperradiant lens, a behemoth of prisms, and magnifying panels weighing 14 tons.

The station was automated in 1974. A few years later, vandals shot a bullet through the valuable lens. Despite the damage, the beacon remains active. The houses were razed in the 1980s.

A narrow, fenced trail leads around the face of lofty Makapu'u Point on windward O'ahu. The squat lighthouse and its powerful beacon provide air and sea landfall. In the 1980s, while Honolulu police conducted target practice on the site, the lens was damaged by a stray bullet. **Both photos:** *Elinor De Wire*

Nāwiliwili Harbor Lighthouse
LIHU'E, KAUA'I

DIRECTIONS
From Highway 50 in Lihu'e, turn right on Rice Street (where Highway 50 becomes Highway 56). Go approximately 1.5 miles down Rice Street and turn left into the lighthouse compound.

A light was established on Kūki'i Point at Nāwiliwili Harbor in 1897 to guide vessels working in the sugar trade on Kaua'i. A 40-foot open-framework wooden tower held a lamp and reflector that sent a beam about 10 miles. The structure was rebuilt again in 1923 and underwent major repair in 1926. The present lighthouse went into service at Ninini Point in 1932 and is an 86-foot reinforced-concrete tower. Its electric beacon projected light for 17 miles. It was automated in 1953. The lantern was later removed and an aerobeacon was installed. The original fourth-order lens is on display at the Hawai'i Maritime Center.

With the burgeoning sugar cane industry on Kaua'i in the 1890s, a good light was needed at Nāwiliwili Harbor. Two wooden lights preceded the current concrete tower on Ninini Point. *U.S. Coast Guard*

For More Information

Dean, Love. *Lighthouses of Hawai'i*. Honolulu, HI: University of Hawaii Press, 1995.

De Wire, Elinor. *Guardians of the Lights: Stories of U.S. Lighthouse Keepers*. Sarasota, FL: Pineapple Press, 1995.

————. *Sentries along the Shore*. Gales Ferry, CT: Sentinel Publications, 1997.

Gibbs, James. *Lighthouses of the Pacific*. West Chester, PA: Schiffer Publishing, 1986.

Leffingwell, Randy, and Pamela Welty. *Lighthouses of the Pacific Coast*. Stillwater, MN: Voyageur Press, 2000.

Lowry, Shannon, and Jeff Schultz. *Northern Lights: Tales of Alaska's Lighthouses and Their Keepers*. Harrisburg, PA: Stackpole Books, 1992.

Nelson, Sharlene, and Ted Nelson. *California Lighthouses*. Portland, OR: Umbrella Books, 1993.

————. *Oregon Lighthouses*. Portland, OR: Umbrella Books, 1994.

————. *Washington Lighthouses*. Portland, OR: Umbrella Books, 1998.

Noble, Dennis. *Lighthouses and Keepers*. Annapolis, MD: Naval Institute Press, 1997.

Roberts, Bruce, and Ray Jones. *Pacific Northwest Lighthouses*. Old Saybrook, CT: Globe Pequot Press, 1997.

Online Sources

American Lighthouse Foundation
P.O. Box 889, Wells, ME 04090,
   phone 207.646.0245
   e-mail alf@lighthousefoundation.org
   visit www.lighthousefoundation.org

U.S. Lighthouse Society
244 Kearny Street, San Francisco, CA 94108,
   phone 415.362.7255
   visit www.uslhs.org

Note: Websites for individual lighthouses are listed within the field guide.

Index

142

About the Author

Elinor De Wire has been researching, photographing, and writing about lighthouses since 1972. She has visited more than eight-hundred sentinels in the U.S., Canada, Mexico, the Caribbean, Europe, and Australia and is the author of eleven books and more than one-hundred articles on the subject.

Audiences from Maine to Hawaii have enjoyed her programs, including the popular "I Brake for Lighthouses," and "Women of the Lights." Her workshops, "Lighthouses on the Beam" and "Lighthouse History & Lore in the Classroom," have been shared with teachers and students in schools and museums around the country. Retired Coast Guard Historian, Dr. Robert Scheina calls Elinor "America's most prolific lighthouse author and a driving force behind the recent upsurge in interest in preserving lighthouses and the history and nostalgia surrounding them."

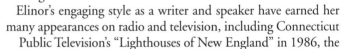

Elinor's engaging style as a writer and speaker have earned her many appearances on radio and television, including Connecticut Public Television's "Lighthouses of New England" in 1986, the University of Wisconsin's "Earthwatch" in 1992, National Public Television's "Legendary Lighthouses" in 1998, and The Learning Channel's "Haunted Lighthouses" in 1998 and 2003. She has worked with the Children's Television Network, the National Park Service, the National Oceanic & Atmospheric Administration, and the D.C. Heath Company to produce lighthouse programs and materials.

Elinor is the founder and charter president of the Washington Lightkeepers Association and an advisory board member for several nonprofit lighthouse groups in her home state. She chairs the American Lighthouse Foundation's youth initiative "Kids on the Beam" and writes a bimonthly column for kids in Lighthouse Digest.

She serves as educational consultant for the Delaware Bay & River Lighthouse Foundation and the Florida Lighthouse Association. She has been honored for her work in journalism, education, and historic preservation by the U.S. Lighthouse Society, the American Association of University Women, the American Lighthouse Foundation, New England Lighthouse Lovers, the Avery Point Lighthouse Society, the Florida Lighthouse Association, and the National League of American Pen Women. Three of her books have won Coast Guard Book Awards and the Ben Franklin Book Award.

Elinor currently is at work on a series of lighthouse guidebooks, plus The Lightkeeper's Menagerie, about lighthouse animals, and Send a Gleam across the Wave: the Story of Washington Lighthouses & Lightships. She resides in Seabeck, Washington with her husband, Jonathan, a retired Navy officer, and her cat, Lighthouse Kitty, the mascot of the American Lighthouse Foundation's Youth Initiative. Her two grown children, Jessica and Scott, have fond memories of the family's many travels to lighthouses.